Medical STORIES &JOKES
for Speakers

NURSE: 'You've got a baby girl.'
HUSBAND (*relieved*): 'Thank goodness for that. She'll never have to go through what I've gone through.'

Medical STORIES & JOKES
for Speakers

Compiled by
Geoffrey Matson

foulsham

LONDON · NEW YORK · TORONTO · SYDNEY

foulsham

Yeovil Road, Slough, Berkshire SL1 4JH

ISBN 0-572-01606-9

Copyright © 1990 Geoffrey J. Matson
Originally published as *Emergency Ward*

Printed in Great Britain by
St Edmundsbury Press Ltd
Bury St Edmunds, Suffolk

I proudly dedicate this book to my wife who has been nursing me patiently through a long and, so far, incurable illness, and who has, herself, been into hospitals six times, often for long duration, and who has undergone two major operations so bravely. God bless her!

CONTENTS

Medical STORIES & JOKES
for Speakers

Foreword

Those who have been into hospital as patients, at one time or another, and the many who have been, or who are still, concerned in some way with the running of such an institution, will know that there must, of necessity, always be an atmosphere of tranquillity, efficiency, and concentration within such a place. Now and again, however, some unexpected incident occurs – often of a humorous nature – which brings smiles to the faces of patients and staff alike. Away from the wards, such incidents are told and re-told especially among Nurses, until soon there are smiles snowballing throughout the whole building.

As a patient I have witnessed some such incidents myself, and I have seen others, or heard of others, when I have been visiting my wife in various wards where she has been undergoing treatment.

It occurred to me that many of these incidents, and others like them, would make interesting reading, and accordingly, I set out to get suitable contributions and form them into a book. At this point I must convey my warm and grateful thanks to the editors of *Nursing Times*, *Nursing Mirror*, and *Midwives' Chronicle*, who were so kind and ready to print a request to their readers to send accounts of their own experiences which might prove suitable for a book of this nature. The response was enormous, and the letters confirmed, what I already knew, how generous and kind-hearted our Nurses are. Many of them spent quite a lot of their spare time sending in material, and the letters accompanying the material often showed how devoted our Nurses are and how much they have the interests of their patients at heart. Truly can it be said that there is no finer band of creatures on God's earth, than Nurses.

Doctors with whom I got into touch were, generally, more serious minded, and, although they could recall incidents of a humorous nature, they much preferred to write on some interesting aspect of medicine itself. This has been a good thing really, since such contributions have enabled me to make my book more generally appealing. As one might suppose of members of this profession, most of the doctors have hidden their real identity under initials or *nom de plumes*. Despite this, however, the contributions are none the less interesting. Most readers, I am sure, will like to know of the origin of some of our best known London hospitals, and many, like me, will doubtless be surprised to learn that two of these hospitals have been treating the sick continuously for over 800 years.

The story of Elizabeth Blackwell is a very fascinating one, and tells of the many enormous obstacles which had to be overcome before the first woman was able to become a successful doctor. Other contributions tell the fascinating stories around vaccination and penicillin, and another tells of the life-long devotion to medicine by John Hunter. All these should prove very encouraging, since they show what a lot of time and thought go into the work of people who are dedicated to medical science. We hear little of this kind of work, from day to day, but there is no doubt that thousands of people the whole world over are always giving unstintingly of their time and talent, to explore some avenue of medicine which at present is partly obscured.

A number of celebrities have kindly supplied contributions of one kind and another, some of which are just jokes with a medical flavour, whilst others are of a more general nature. Richard Gordon, for instance, author of the now famous 'Doctor' books, tells how he first became interested in writing these; Vivian Ellis describes how some of his biggest successes came when he was feeling unwell; and Godfrey Winn, in his own inimitable style, gives a graphic account of how a patient gave him a fresh outlook on life and work altogether.

I have tried to take all these various ingredients at my disposal and make them up into a palatable mixture which can be taken as 'doses of medicine' to bring fun and interest to all who read them. I hope you will consider I have been successful in doing just this.

Geoffrey J. Matson.

My Dose of 'Doctors'

I decided to give up practising as a Doctor for writing about them in the middle of the Tropic of Cancer – not Henry Miller's, but the real one, which in mid-July is even hotter. I was the Doctor aboard a cargo ship bound for Australia, and it seemed nobody dared to fall ill. My duties were reduced to drinking gin with the Chief Engineer and hearing his touching stories of lovely rain-washed nights in Glasgow, which was as nice a way of passing the time as any, but seemed liable to end me up with one of those livers they pass across the table in a glass jar during the pathology exams.

As a change from gin and Glasgow, I set up my portable typewriter in the shadiest corner of the deck and decided to write a book. I'd had a bit of experience in this line, having just finished a job on one of the clinical journals. The editor put me in charge of the obituaries, which was valuable training. It taught me to write convincing fiction. On one afternoon I killed off a Doctor of Divinity by mistake and shortly afterwards found myself free to go to sea.

The book I had in mind was something of a cross between *War and Peace* and Gray's *Anatomy*. As my life had been spent almost exclusively in the company of Doctors, Medical Students, Nurses, patients, and corpses, I couldn't write about anything at all except my own profession. I didn't intend *Doctor in the House* to be funny, but set out to describe doctors as they really were while learning the job, and it sort of turned out that way. I reckoned the proceeds might run to a second-hand car. My publisher put them at a de-coke for his Bentley.

My characters have now been portrayed so magnificently by actors like Mr. Dirk Bogarde and Mr. James Robertson Justice, I've long forgotten who's which. Did I ever think of Sir Lancelot Spratt as a bearded surgical bear? And Simon Sparrow as a good-looking chap with a flair for female cardiology? I don't know.

And I've now written so many books about doctors, I find I type sentences, paragraphs, and even whole chapters I've written once before. Odd. Perhaps it's time for me to go back and chum up with that Chief Engineer once more!

Richard Gordon.
(Copyright Richard Gordon Ltd.)

Old Danny

Two circles of white light on the ceiling from the reflection of the night light, and a glow over the centre table, was all the light in the ward. The Staff Nurse had pulled down the centre light and draped a green frill round it, so that its light was confined to a small area in the centre of the table, where Staff could do her writing.

The silence which reigned both within and without, was broken only by a distant clock striking the hour of one. A few minutes later, however, a slight rat-tat sound came from somewhere much nearer.

Staff looked up. 'That will be Old Danny,' she murmured, and picking up her torch she made her way to the bed from whence the sound came.

Old Danny was quite a well-known character in the ward. He was a tall, spare old man, nearly blind, and getting on for seventy. He suffered from an aneurysm, and came into the ward at regular intervals for a check-up.

'What's wrong, Danny,' whispered Staff, 'do you want something?'

'I'm seeking for me pipe,' said the old man. 'I want a wee puff.'

'But Danny, it's the middle of the night, you can't smoke just now,' Staff replied.

'Oh, I just want three draws to make me sleep,' urged Danny.

'Hush, Danny, you'll be waking everyone up, and you really can't smoke just now. The Night Sister will be coming round any minute now, and she will be furious if she finds you smoking.'

'I'll hide the pipe when she comes,' argued Danny.

'That's no use,' said Staff, 'she'll be sure to smell it, and I'll get into an awful row. I will get you a nice cup of tea and that will help you to sleep.'

'I dinna want any tea,' said Danny, getting quite annoyed. 'I just want a wee draw.'

'Hush! hush! Danny, listen, I'll tell you what I'll do. You let me shake up your pillows and make you comfortable. Then I'll give you a peppermint to suck, and you can lie back and count sheep going through a gap, and as soon as Sister has been round, I'll let you have a wee draw.'

Danny grunted, but he leaned forward and let Staff rearrange his pillows. Then he lay back and closed his eyes but he would not have a peppermint.

'I've settled him for the time being,' thought Staff, going back to her assistant. 'But I don't know for how long.'

It was about a quarter of an hour later that another faint sound alerted the Nurses – the slight squeak of a door. 'It's the Sister,' hissed the Assistant Nurse. Staff Nurse rose, and hanging her red cape over the back of her chair, she went down the ward to meet the tall figure in navy blue who was gliding noiselessly towards her. They went on their round talking in very subdued voices.

As they approached Danny's bed, Staff said, 'We have got Old Danny in again.'

'Poor old man,' said Sister, 'I'm glad to see he is resting so quietly.' No sooner were the words out of her mouth than Danny's long arm waved in the air, and he half raised himself up in the bed.

The Night Sister stepped forward and patted his hand. 'Well, Danny, how are you?' she asked. 'Is there anything you want?'

Danny grasped her hand, pulled her slowly towards him, and

in a loud stage whisper said: 'Has the auld bitch been round yet?'

Staff wished the floor would open and swallow her up but the Sister gave Danny's head another gentle pat, and turning to Staff she said: 'I'm afraid the old man is wandering a bit. See if you can soothe him, Nurse. Your assistant can continue the round with me.'

Miss J. E. Douglas.

Pregnancy Responsibilities

Extract from an essay written by a nurse in training

A woman who is expecting a baby should always go to her local Doctor as soon as she has reason to believe that she may be pregnant. She must realize that her local Doctor is always the person mainly responsible for her condition.

D. C. F.

The Heavenly Banjo

I was nursing during the war on a very busy male surgical ward. In one corner was a French Colonial sailor of Negro origin who was the only one left of many refugees who had passed through the ward. He was very lonely, and in an effort to cheer him up, some of his friends had brought him in a banjo which he was always playing. On one particular afternoon, he was strumming away when one of the English soldiers, a fair, blue-eyed army sergeant, was brought back into the ward from the operating theatre. Screens were placed round the bed whilst, from the corner, came the strains of the Colonial's banjo. At length the blue-eyed sergeant slowly opened his eyes, looked at me wonderingly, and exclaimed 'Good Gawd – I thought I was in heaven till I saw you!'

Mrs. S. F. Mitcham.

SISTER (*to man who has been visiting his twin brother*): 'What are *you* doing out here. Come back to bed with me at once!'

A Hospital Maid's Dilemma

Poor Martha was broke, she lamented,
As there on the sofa she lay.
She had come to the end of her wages,
And there she was, off for the day.

The Nurses were all sympathetic,
They loaned her a gold fountain pen,
Advised her to try it at Uncle's,
For Martha was lucky with men.

So Martha went round to the pawn-shop,
The pen on the counter was laid,
'Here's ten and a kick, dear,' said Uncle,
And promptly the money was paid.

Pay day came round on the Friday,
And Martha remembered the pen,
But she just couldn't find the darn ticket,
Though she hunted again and again.

Then Martha was called to the office,
She arrived in the queue about nine,
Like some poor erring soul at the Sessions,
Prepared for a sentence or fine.

But Matron could scarcely help laughing,
'Do you recognize this?' she said.
'It was found in your coat at the laundry,'
And Martha said, 'Pinch me, I'm dead!'

There was joy in heaven with the angels,
There was joy in the Home and around,
The prayers of the Nurses were answered.
For Martha's pawn ticket was found.

*　　*　　*

Beyond the Limelight

The Administrative Sisters, they are working day and night,
To organize more smoothly a world that won't go right
Unless they help to make it. They plan and pour the oil
That smoothes a sea of troubles for lesser folk who toil.

The patients seldom meet them, but the bed-side needs they know,
Having worked the wards in training not so very long ago.
Like good administrators they stand beyond the glow
Of each day's nursing limelight, but they surely make things go!

So you're back from holiday and find you're 'on' tonight,
Don't wonder if the name is wrong, (you bet they've got it right!)
Or feel that in some game of chance you're just another pawn;
The Administrative Sisters to chance anything would scorn.

When they attain to heaven, as I'm sure at length they will,
And find a neat salvation on its tidy little hill,
To see the place well organized should fill their hearts with zest,
While from other people's duties may the saints prescribe a rest!

J. R. Butler.

He Wasn't Experiencing It

I was doing a show in a hospital some time ago and was quoting several catch phrases from my current *Ray's A Laugh* show.

Unknown to me, some patient was being given an enema at the other end of the ward, and whether or not the mixture was too hot, I do not know, but suddenly a blood-curdling yell rang out and another patient shouted 'IT's LUVLY, MRS. HOSKIN . . . IT's LUVLY.'

Ted Ray.

How to Enjoy Ill-Health

It is quite possible to enjoy ill-health. I have been enjoying ill-health for years. All through the writing of *Mr. Cinders* I was seriously ill, yet I composed the song 'Spread a little Happiness' between attacks of vomiting, and with a temperature of 103 degrees.

I had jaundice right through *Going Places* and missed the first night at the Savoy Theatre – which was perhaps as well, as the show was a flop. I had raging toothache during all the rehearsals of *Big Ben* and so did my collaborator, Sir Alan Herbert, yet, between visits to our dentists, we managed to produce a song entitled 'I want to see the People Happy'.

To return to ill-health. There are one or two obstacles a patient must surmount before he can extract the fullest enjoyment from his infirmities. First, he must be able to survive treatment from Doctors. This requires a great deal of physical and mental strength, but it can be done. There are thousands of people walking about this country today who have managed to outlive treatment by Doctors, Surgeons, and even physiotherapists and osteopaths. Years of our English climate and hotel cooking, have given us a stamina that is the envy of all but a Chinese yak.

More difficult to cope with are Nurses, especially Commonwealth Nurses in one's home, unless one is keen on studying geography, the taking of coloured photos and the day-to-day goings-on of our Royal Family. Yet there are several homes that have not yet been broken up by the arrival of the Commonwealth Nurse (and the departure of the resident domestic staff or daily help).

Should, however, one's illness coincide with a social function such as a Royal wedding, Ascot, or a State procession in the Mall, the patient must be prepared to fend for himself until a nurse is available.

Some of the advantages of ill-health are the boring acts one is no longer compelled to perform, such as receiving relations ('I'm sorry, he's resting'), weeding the garden (I mustn't bend), washing up (I'm not allowed to stand), in fact, any sort of domestic chore. Nor is one obliged to join in parlour games (I can't concentrate), amuse the children (they make too much noise), answer the telephone or watch the telly – except, of course, for the more bloodthirsty hospital programmes.

During your disability you should receive, in addition to your sickness benefit, the best cuts and portions, the choicest dessert, and the most comfortable chair. You should be served first and awakened last, preferably with breakfast in bed on a tray, or if later in the day, with a nice hot cup of tea and a book.

All news of a disastrous nature should be withheld from you, but if, by some unfortunate chance, you are told that the daily woman has walked out, your wife has fallen down or your children have all contracted measles, you should immediately feign sleep. Make the most of your rest while you can get it, for very soon it will be your turn to wait upon the next lucky person enjoying the relaxation of ill-health.

Vivian Ellis.

Poor Sucker!

Smiles flicker across the faces of Doctors and Nurses alike in most hospitals, from time to time, when someone comes across a good example of the unconscious humour which turns up occasionally, in the notes kept on patients by the person in charge of the ward at the time.

I have heard many examples of this kind, but three which have always stuck in my memory, and which make me smile whenever I think of them, are the following:

'Mrs. —— ate a little jelly; vomited a trifle.'

'Betty —— has been vomiting frequently all day. I understand she is expecting her sister up this evening.'

'Mrs. —— doing well, but baby not so good. Taking breast badly. Poor sucker!'

Staff Nurse, Stoke Mandeville.

One Pair of Hands

(With apologies to Monica Dickens)

Nurse, Nurse, please come quickly,
Number Ten is feeling sickly,
Number Seven is on the floor,
Now there's Matron at the door.

Nurse, please hurry with the trolley
Our diabetic has a lolly,
Number eight has gastric flu,
Number three is turning blue.

Nurse, can I have a drink of water?
Hurry up and fetch a porter,
Have you done the dressings, Staff?
I feel as if I'm sawn in half.

Nurse, will you get the screens?
The gastric case is eating beans,
Help Staff do the pressure points,
Then give heat to swollen joints.

Nurse, have you seen that sleeping beauty?
It's nearly time to go off duty.
Give the patients morning drinks,
Then go and clean the sluice and sinks.

Nurses should be clean and neat,
Seams all straight, and dainty feet,
All these things and many more,
One pair of hands, what joys in store?

Margaret J. White.

Doses of Death

'More than 10,500 dangerous barbiturate tablets were stolen from a chemist's shop at Chesterfield, Derbyshire, yesterday. The tablets could be a fatal dose.'

Just about, I should think!

News Item from Daily Express.

Not What He Expected

Although I am only a Student Nurse in my third year, I have come across many humorous incidents, although it is not always easy to think of them on the spur of the moment. The following two, however, are fresh in my memory.

The Nurse in charge was doing her ward before settling patients for the night, and to one, who was rather breathless, she decided to give him some special suppositories to help his breathing.

While she was in the process, the patient exclaimed indignantly, 'Nurse, what are you doing? It's not me bowels, it's me lungs!'

The other concerns a very new Probationer Nurse who was assisting the Doctor with the taking of a patient's blood for testing. I must explain here that there is a special crystal substance in the bottom of the blood bottle for chemical reasons.

Sensing the Nurse seemed rather active, the Doctor asked, 'Nurse, what are you doing?'

'Oh, sir,' came the reply, 'just blowing the dust out of the bottle!'

J. C. Sceats.

Mother's Bad Day

It really needs a Scotsman to tell the story of the old Scottish lady – bed-ridden, but strong-minded – who lived in a village, looked after by her daughter.

There was only one thing they disagreed on: whenever the mother had a bad day (as old people do at times), she would say, 'Send for the Minister' – and rather reluctantly, the daughter did as she was told.

For family reasons they had occasion to move away to a wee house in another village, and the daughter thought: 'This is my chance – I'll have no more nonsense; the next time mother has a bad turn, it's the Doctor I'll be sending for, not the Minister. Mother won't know; they dress very much alike.'

Sure enough, before long the old lady felt a bit off colour, and the daughter called in the Doctor. He came – and went.

After she had seen him out she went up to her mother's room and said: 'Well, Mother, don't you think he did you a bit of good?' 'Yes, indeed he did,' agreed the old lady. 'Well, there you are, Mother, it was the Doctor, and not the Minister at all.'

'Ah, now,' said the old lady. 'That explains it. You know, for a Minister, I thought he was a wee bit – familiar.'

Rex Palmer.

An Expert Diagnosis

A medical story I find amusing is the following:

A gardening enthusiast decided to cultivate some fruit and bought a collection of trees of various kinds. He planted them and watched their progress carefully. He became concerned about a tree that seemed to be making little progress and he asked his neighbour, an obstetrician at the local hospital, to give his opinion. The neighbour studied the tree for several minutes before announcing solemnly: 'It is a little early for diagnosis, but there is every indication that it is going to have a damson.'

Comedian *Freddie Sales.*

An Unusual Operation

I am a disabled Nurse living in a bungalow on a council estate. I find that life is never dull if one is willing to enter into the happenings around. It is seldom that I spend a whole day without a call for help of some kind. Casualties are mostly of a minor nature though we do sometimes have more serious accidents. As this is a country area and I have a telephone, it is nearly always from here that the message requesting help is sent. It may be for the Doctor, Midwife, or in the case of accidents, the police.

It came as no surprise, then, to find a lady on my doorstep one evening, asking for help. 'Can you 'elp me?' she queried.

'Why, yes, of course, if I can,' I said. 'Come in.'

She came in, and information regarding her trouble came slowly. 'I've bin potato picking,' she said.

'Yes, I know. Is there something wrong?'

'I've 'ad a haccident.'

I looked vainly for signs of blood or a bandage; but there was nothing to indicate the nature of this accident. I could only assume she had perhaps acquired a hernia from lifting a sack of potatoes. 'Well, what has happened?' I asked.

Imagine my surprise when she produced a pair of tartan trews torn from the band to the gusset. 'Do you think you could mend them for me?' she ventured. 'You see, every time the farmer came up the field today, I 'ad to turn the other way.'

Needless to say, she got her stitches – but not surgical ones.

Miss E. J. Slatter.

A Business Proposition

My wife spent several months in a large provincial hospital and, during this time, among the Nurses who looked after her was a young girl who was exceedingly kind and very cheerful. She had a keen sense of humour and quietly made jokes with the various patients as she flitted from bed to bed carrying out her several duties. Everyone liked her and her keen sense of humour was widely appreciated.

I chanced to meet her on several occasions when I was visiting my wife, and we usually had a laugh about something. I, too, have a keen sense of humour – although some, at times, may think a little distorted – and when I visited my wife on the last occasion before she came out, Nurse was saying how much she was going to miss her. We live in a comparatively small town which, despite its size, has a very large market on Mondays and, apart from the livestock, there are always a number of stalls and other attractions in the market place. People naturally crowd in, and when Nurse said she would like to come and visit us some-time, I suggested she should try to come on market day, when there was always plenty to see.

'That sounds a good idea,' said the Nurse, 'and if there are all the people you say, it might be a good idea to come and set up a bed-pan service.' For some reason or other bed-pans always seem good enough for a laugh in hospitals.

Coming home from seeing my wife, I thought of this idea of Nurse's, and thought it might be fun sending her a letter out-lining such an idea. Accordingly, when I got back, I sent the following, and I understand it has caused many a titter among those who have read it.

Dear Nurse,

I have been thinking carefully over the proposition you made when I saw you on Saturday, and I think we might very easily make a successful business venture on the lines you suggested. Accordingly, I have gone into the matter very carefully, and I estimate that, for a second-hand van, a luxury commode, a sufficient supply of bed-pans, bottles and paper, we should require approximately £4000. If you can persuade your father to put up £3500 of this amount – and I'm quite sure he will be happy to assist you – I will willingly put up the balance myself. We can then get into business and be ready to start operations on Easter Monday.

I think the wording for the van is suitable as you suggested and we might have it painted as follows:

JOHNSON & BATES
BED-PAN SERVICE
Use of Luxury Commode, £2.50
Use of Bed-Pan, £1.25
Use of Bottle, 40p
Enemas by appointment

I have spoken to the Chairman of the Market Committee and he has very kindly promised to allocate us a prominent place. I have also had a word with His Worship the Mayor, and he has graciously consented to come and perform the opening ceremony. This will almost certainly lead to a picture in the local paper which will get us a lot of publicity. I am also thinking it would be a good idea to have some toilet rolls specially printed and then you or Mrs. Bates could stand by the side of the van and tear a piece off and hand to passers-by. The wording for these rolls needs some thought, but I think you may agree that the following may be suitable:

YOU MAY NEED THIS!
If you do, come to the bed-pan service.
Service with Comfort
All operations carried out under the personal supervision
of a trained Nurse.
'Comfort' is our motto.

I have written to two or three of the manufacturers of toilet papers, to see if I can induce one of them to give us free gifts for the first fifty or one hundred customers, say, a bottle of castor oil or a packet of Epsom salts, or some other equally delicious stimulant. I feel sure they will respond, but we shall, of course, have to guarantee to use their products exclusively.

I have also spoken to a millinery friend of mine who has promised to design an attractive form of head-dress based on the shape of a bed-pan. I have no doubt you will be proud to wear this.

We must get together sometime to discuss the sharing of profits, although I expect you, like me, feel that profits are only of secondary consideration. What must come first is the comfort of the masses – particularly in the plum season!

If this service proves successful – and I am quite sure it will – we can think of extending it further by arranging to visit fêtes, garden parties, barbecues, and the like. In fact, we could be ready to go anywhere where there is a need – and where is there where there is not a need!

Joking apart, I am really writing to thank you so very much for being kind and cheerful to Mrs. Bates when she was with you. Your happy manner really did do her a power of good.

Yours sincerely,
A Patient's Husband.

The Meaning of Words

It is a very long time since I practised medicine and I seem to have forgotten the funniest incidents of my medical career, but two I do remember are the interesting diagnoses that patients made upon themselves.

I was called out one night at the request of a small girl who had been sent with a message which was: 'Would you please come quick, Doctor, as mother has got bronkits on the chest.' This on discovery, turned out to be bronchitis on the chest.

The other one was a very small girl who arrived with a message which again said: 'Please come quickly, Tommy's legs is hysterical.' I did go quickly, but never did discover what was wrong with Tommy's legs!

Lady Isobel Barnett.

An Interesting Demonstration

A senior consultant came to a hospital in which I was working, to do a teaching round in a ward full of patients suffering from tuberculosis. There were several medical students who had come to listen, and Sister said the Nurses who were on duty might listen also.

We dutifully trailed after the great man, hanging upon every word. Among other things, he explained about the detection of fluid levels in the chest, and we were shown X-ray pictures of this. Then he said it was possible to assess this clinically by actually shaking the patient (a short rapid movement), and listening for a splash with a stethoscope. He demonstrated this, and then asked one of the medical students to try it. The student did so, then stepped back into place saying: 'Oh, yes! Very obvious, couldn't miss hearing it.'

'Well,' said the cockney voice of the patient, ''e ought to. I was 'olding me 'ot water bottle!'

Kathleen Press.

The Eye Bandage

I was on night duty on my own on the Ophthalmic Ward, which was divided into two parts, with the men in one half and the women in the other. At this particular time we had a male patient who had undergone an operation for cataract, and was not very good for keeping his eye bandage on. As I was going round, I noticed his bandage was very much out of place and that he was pulling at it in his sleep. I went to him and tried to straighten the bandage and also to stop him from uncovering the eye. Whilst I did this, I spoke to him, and tried to reassure him, but he was having none of my help. He fought me, lashing out with his fists, and calling out loudly for me to go away. The commotion woke the rest of the ward, and the patient was proving so difficult that another man in the ward had to come to my assistance.

Eventually, he quietened down, and as he became fully aware of his surroundings he turned to me and said: 'Sorry, Nurse, I thought it was my wife!'

We were all amused by this remark, and when we told his wife, she took it good-humouredly and said, 'He often fights in bed if I disturb him.'

Susan K. Chaffin.

Bronchitis Cure

I could feel the cold wind searching the very marrow of my bones as we cycled along the road that Sunday, but I had been free of sniffles and sneezes so long, that I didn't worry unduly. The sky looked ominous, but the countryside was lovely, and I was easily persuaded to go home by a longer route, although by this time I was really chilled.

A hot bath before going to bed was as much as I could bother taking, and in the morning, the worst had begun. My chest felt as tight as a drum, my eyes curiously unwilling to open, and there was a horrid lassitude in every limb. I knew I had a show on Wednesday, but this was only Monday, and all might yet be well.

I decided against doing the washing – too strenuous. Still, I couldn't sit all day doing nothing, for I didn't feel really ill. My eye lighted on the kitchen walls – this might be a good time leisurely to remove the grey look, when I had nothing else to do. I collected my equipment and set to work. I washed them, and I dried them, and then found that the floor looked a bit grimy against the sparkling shine of the walls. The floor was duly washed, then polished, and then it seemed sort of silly not to do the rest of the linoleum while I had the polish in my hands, and before I knew where I was, I had polished every surface in the entire house.

After that, what could be more natural than to get the duster out and make the furniture match the floors. It seemed a pity too, not to Hoover the carpets while the power was there, for there was sure to be a cut in the morning and I wouldn't be able to do the carpets then.

The man of the house was a little late in getting home, so I thought I might as well make a little pastry whilst I was waiting. I couldn't settle somehow, an ominous sign, and I might have realized I was running a temperature. In fact, I was rather sorry now that I had cravenly decided against tackling the washing; there wasn't much to it really, but I agreed with myself, rather reluctantly, that it was a bit late to start it at this hour of the day.

Bed was torture. I seemed to be two people, one lying awake and watchful, lest the drowsy one choke from the tightness of that chest, and the other desperate for sleep, but unable to drop off because the first one kept jogging her awake each time she drifted away.

Next morning, Tuesday, found me with a voice like broken glass, a feverish brow, and a very worried mind.

I began drinking emulsion, which up till now had never failed me, but this time it had no effect. I felt my bronchitis was now a tangible enemy, that battle must be enjoined, and I threw everything I had into the attack.

I took my husband's old cough bottle before lunch; emulsion before tea; the man next door's cough bottle before supper; inhaled with friar's balsam; drank the remains of an old bottle of linctus which had been prescribed a year before for someone else; took two Anadins, two Alka-Seltzers, sipped whisky and hot water and sugar – in fact the wicked lot!

Wednesday dawned bright and clear, after a terrible night of throbbing perspiration and hacking coughing; but the enemy, while it hadn't entirely left the battlefield, was definitely on the run. My voice was now romantically deep and husky, but audible, and a slight moistness round my eyes and forehead were the only visible signs of the ordeal I had been through.

We went on the air as scheduled, and my voice nobly rose to the occasion, with only the very faintest indication of hoarseness.

However, thanks to all the remedies I tried, I shall never know what cured me.

Was it the friar's balsam?

Was it the neighbour's cough bottle?

Was it my husband's cough cure?

Was it the linctus?

Could it have been the Anadins? Or the Alka-Seltzers?

Or maybe the whisky and sugar? Or perhaps the emulsion?

Who knows? I don't.

It's an appalling thought, but if I take a cold this winter (touch wood), I shall just have to try the whole assortment again. Boy, pass me my cold-preventive tablets! Mmm, very good!

Molly W. Weir.

A Helpful Flower

I was doing the round of the ward one morning and asking the familiar questions quietly of one patient, 'What about the bowels dear,' (those who have been patients in hospitals will know that this is one of the questions asked regularly every morning), and this particular patient replied in a loud voice, for all to hear, 'I've just 'ad an anemone! I feel fine!'

Marion Criston.

34

DOCTOR'S DAUGHTER: 'Is it true, Mother, that storks bring babies?'
DOCTOR'S WIFE: 'You had better ask Daddy, dear, I know he helps deliver
them.'

Doses I Remember

I have left active nursing now and am married, and the only doses of medicine I give are to my own little children. There are, however, two occasions of doses of medicine which I gave in my nursing days, which, for quite different reasons, have always remained in my memory.

On the first occasion I was told to go to a poor old lady who had just been brought into the general ward and give her a dose of paraffin oil. I did not relish this very much, since I had already been told that the patient herself had been a Matron in her day. When I approached her with the bottle and spoon, she mumbled something hardly intelligible, and I took it she was prepared to refuse the medicine.

I worried about this, since all nurses naturally respect someone who has been a Matron, and I felt I should hate to have to contradict her. I said all the usual things. 'It is good for you, it is very gentle, I'll help you to swallow it,' and so on, but she kept mumbling and, to add to my distress, would not open her mouth wide enough for me to give her the spoon. At length she opened her weary eyes as much as she could, and gave me a very appealing look. With a supreme effort, she said, sufficiently clearly to understand: 'If it is an oil, always put a little water on the spoon first, then the oil won't stick.'

This poor old lady always gives me a thrill of love when I think of her. With her inbred sense of good nursing, she was able to teach still, and once more in her last days, she was able to give me a lesson which taught me much more than simply putting water under oils.

My other story concerns a village pharmacist and morphia. By the time this happened, I was Sister-in-Charge of a T.B. sanatorium. Most of the patients were convalescent but one had occasionally to have a dose of morphia to check bleeding. We had no tablets immediately to hand, and whenever we were short of a drug, we always went into the nearest town to get a new supply. On this occasion, however, I did not wish to spare the time to go into town, and decided to go to the local pharmacist in the village, since the phial of tablets I had was almost empty.

The local pharmacy belonged to a kindly old pharmacist, and his middle-aged daughter helped around the shop and kept house for him in the adjoining room. I rarely went to this shop, as our needs were quite high, and we had a credit account at the pharmacy in town.

I presented my prescription, and he read it and said: 'Morphia, urgent', whilst searching amongst the stock. He closed the poison cupboard and went to another. No luck. He tried another corner, but there was still no sign of the drug. Off he trundled to find his daughter. He returned with poor hopes, but with a torch in hand. I had hoped to save time, but the waiting still went on. Together they searched all the corners again with the torch, but still with no luck. At last, however, the search proved fruitful, and out from behind some bottles and jars, emerged a dusty and old phial.

My prescription had asked for twenty tablets, and the old man took out the contents to check. To his sorrow, there were only seventeen tablets. He packed them in again, and altering the prescription, he told me: 'There are only seventeen left, there has been such a run on them recently!' I kept my face straight, but when I left the shop, I had to burst out laughing. Then I realized his little lie had saved the situation; the long period of waiting had been made worth while after all.

Eva Cahn, S.R.N., S.C.M., Haifa, Israel.

Two Golden Screws

Hello, my darlings! Do you like a silly story? I do, and although the following is very silly, it always seems to make people laugh.

A man woke up one morning, jumped out of bed, looked in

the mirror, and noticed that he had a golden screw sticking out of each ear. He hastily dressed himself and raced off to see his doctor.

His Doctor had a good look at him, chatted with him for a few minutes, and then sat thinking a little while. Eventually he said: 'I'm sorry, but your condition seems to baffle me a little. I have never seen anything quite like this before. The best thing I can do, is to send you along to see a Golden Screw Earhole Specialist.'

He gave the patient an address, and the man went off to see the specialist.

The latter gave him a careful examination, stroked his chin thoughtfully, and then said: 'There is only one certain cure for a condition such as yours. You must go home and place a bed against a window facing south so that it gets the full rays of the sun. As soon as the sun shines, lie on the bed and let its rays shine down on to your head.'

The man went home, arranged a bed as he had been told, and waited for the sun to shine. When it did, he got on to the bed and let the sun shine full on to his face. He was amazed to see that, before long, a little fairy ran down one of the rays and hopped on to his left ear. It took a small screwdriver from underneath its arm, and carefully unscrewed the screw in that ear. Then it tripped lightly across his forehead, and unscrewed the screw in the other ear. It put the screwdriver back under one arm, the two golden screws under the other arm, hopped back on to the sun's ray and gradually disappeared up it.

The man was amazed to see all this, and tried to sit up a little, the better able to see the fairy's disappearance – *when the back o his head fell off!*

Charlie Drake.

A Nurse Remembers

My adult life has been taken up solely with nursing, and now that I have retired, I can look back on many interesting, and sometimes amusing, incidents which happened during my years in hospital, and later as a District Nurse in places as far apart as the West Country, and the East End of London during the dark days of the war. Let me tell you a few of these incidents.

The Red Flannel Knickers

When I was a Student Nurse in a women's medical ward in my training school, we had a Sister who was very kind to the patients, but who always seemed to we nurses as something of a 'she-dragon'.

On one occasion when I was on duty, an old lady was admitted suffering from bronchitis. The old dear was wearing a weird collection of petticoats, a pair of red flannel knickers, and, last but not least, had a linseed poultice bandaged on her chest. It had been heated and re-heated many times. I washed her and made her comfortable with a hot water bottle.

'Now, my dear,' she said, 'I must have my flannel drawers on.'

I explained to her that this sort of thing was not allowed and told her she could have as many blankets as she wished. As I left her to go on with my other duties, however, I sensed that she was not really satisfied.

Shortly afterwards her Doctor came up to examine her, accompanied by Sister. I walked meekly behind them ready to fetch and carry anything which might be required.

Coming up to her bed, I was asked to turn down the bed clothes, and when I had done this, I discovered, to my dismay, that the old lady had taken the opportunity, whilst I was busy in another part of the ward, of putting on her red flannel knickers. I did not know where to look!

Sister gazed at me very angrily and exclaimed, 'Really, Nurse, I am surprised at you.'

Fortunately, the Doctor was a very sympathetic and understanding man. He turned to Sister and said, 'Sister, don't be cross with Granny or Nurse, perhaps one day you, yourself, will be glad to wear flannel drawers in bed.'

Sister's expression was a study, and to appreciate the situation properly, one had to know that she was the last word in primness – a typical Victorian specimen of the nursing profession.

A Strange Lodging

Two young Student Nurses were due for one night, and two days off duty, and being great friends, they decided to go off somewhere together.

As usual, funds were low, so it must be reasonably near to hospital. They finally decided to go to a watering place about thirty miles away and spend the night at a hostel.

Cook gave them a large packet of mutton sandwiches and off they went. Alas! everything went wrong from the start. It began to rain, the wind got up, and it became very cold. The cinemas were not open until six o'clock, and to top everything the younger of the two began to feel very sick due to having eaten too much fat in her mutton sandwiches. Her companion fetched her a cup of hot tea, hoping it would settle the nausea, but the poor girl only became worse, and said at last 'I am so sorry, but I cannot go on, do find a room and a bed somewhere.'

A policeman was standing at the corner of the road, so her companion asked him if he could direct them to a nice clean house which gave bed and breakfast. He pointed to a large semi-detached house standing back in a garden. She thanked him and fetched her friend.

They rang the bell and this was promptly answered by a stern looking woman wearing a uniform.

Without asking them their business, she said: 'Come in quietly, and don't forget to wipe your boots on the mat.'

She took them up to a long room containing six beds with curtains between each one and said, 'You can get into bed, and tomorrow at seven o'clock, when the bell rings, you get up and follow the other girls.'

The younger girl was thankful to go to bed; the other was hungry and would have loved a cup of tea and a cigarette. No food was forthcoming, however, so she read the detective story she had brought with her, and at last went to sleep. She was only vaguely aware of other girls coming up during the night. They were very quiet, and no words were spoken.

At seven o'clock, they both rose when the bell sounded, the sick girl now being quite recovered. They were conscious of very curious looks in their direction by about twenty young girls.

After a very plain breakfast consisting of porridge, bread and margarine, and tea, they asked the stern looking uniformed woman for their bill. Much to their surprise she suddenly burst out laughing, and when she had heard their story, she said, 'Really, I do apologize. I did not think you were the type. It was next door where you should have gone. This is a home for fallen girls.'

It turned out that the rather poker-faced female was a great friend of their Matron, and they had, in fact, trained together. She gave them a very nice lunch, and when they returned to hospital they found she had phoned their own Matron and told her everything. It was many a long day, however, before the poor girls heard the last of their escapade.

When Ignorance is Bliss

Two women were chatting together in Out-Patients, each one trying to make the other know how much illness her man had suffered at various times. At length, one said, 'My man has a foreign disease now.'

'Oh,' said the other, 'has he been to foreign parts?'

'Not at all,' was the reply, 'I just copied it off his Doctor's certificate. See, I have written it down so that I do not forget the name.' Then she slowly spelt out Ergophobia – which simply means, of course, 'afraid of work'.

Not her Son

Nearly every woman, older than a teenager, in the West Country, always seems to be addressed as 'Ma'.

41

A Sister at the hospital at which I was working had been presented with a young puppy, and she went into the town to buy a tin of dog meat. She paid for it, and received from the young assistant a hearty 'Thanks, Ma'.

Sister, a very prim person, looked searchingly at the assistant and said, very clearly and loudly, 'Young man, I have no recollection of having given birth to you.'

The Stray Dog

This story does not come within my own experience, but was told to me by a Nurse, whose word I never had any reason to doubt. To say the least, it is very mystifying.

As a District Nurse, she was returning from a maternity case at two a.m. when there was a full moon, and it was a bright and frosty night. Suddenly, and without any apparent reason, her car stopped. She got out but found nothing to account for the car's behaviour. Then, out of the blue, a large black dog appeared. It stood still and looked at Nurse. She was a great dog lover and said, 'Good old boy', at the same time stroking it. The dog gave her coat a gentle pull and whined piteously. Nurse thought it must want something, and so she decided to follow it to see what happened. The dog seemed satisfied, and trotted along with Nurse behind, until they stopped outside a little thatched cottage.

Nurse went to the door and knocked. A lamp was burning downstairs but there was no sound. 'Whatever has happened?' she thought. She gave another knock, and when no reply came, she went in. When her eyes had grown accustomed to the dim light, she saw an old lady on the floor wedged between a large table and a chest of drawers. The old lady gave a low moan and said, 'Who are you? I have hurt my leg and cannot get up. I fell off a chair trying to hang up my washing.'

'All right, dear,' said Nurse, 'I will help you, don't worry.' She looked at the leg and suspected a fracture.

'I'm going to phone from the kiosk for an ambulance, and a

doctor will soon come,' she said. She got through to the Doctor and the ambulance, and returned to the cottage. 'Now,' she said, 'I will get things ready for you to take to hospital, and give that nice dog of yours a meal. I will look after him at my own place, until you are able to come home. I love dogs.'

The old lady gave her a bright smile and said, 'I do thank you, Nurse, but Scott, the dog, will not come back; you see he died five years ago, but he always comes back when I need help. When I fell down, he suddenly appeared and sat by me to keep me warm until he went and brought you here.'

To Keep out the Cold

I had a friend who was the District Nurse in a remote but busy district up in the Quantocks.

When war was declared, she told the visiting officer she was willing to take a mother and child into her bungalow, since it was her own and had nothing to do with District Nursing. She told the officer she had no time to look after them, unless, of course, they were sick, but that they were welcome to make full use of the bungalow, and take what fruit and vegetables they required from the garden.

When the mother arrived to settle in she brought with her a little boy of six. Her other two children had been billeted at a farm in Devon, and her husband was serving in France.

They were real cockneys and a little difficult for an Irish Nurse to understand. The day they arrived was very hot, and the journey from London had been very long and tiring. Nurse set out to make them feel welcome, and took to the little boy straight away. She suggested they had a meal at once and said that after the meal the little boy might like a bath and go to bed. The mother looked a bit aghast at this suggestion and exclaimed, 'Have a bath indeed! he'll have nothing of the sort, I have just prepared our Joe for the winter.'

'What have you done, then?' asked Nurse.

'Look, I will show you.' She undressed the child and revealed

43

his body covered all over with brown paper which she had stuck on.

Nurse finally persuaded her to remove it, and Joe got his bath. He is now grown up and in the Navy, but whenever he gets leave he always finds time to visit the nurse who he always refers to as 'his second mother'.

Our Jane

It is many years since I first met Jane. She arrived as a Probationer at the same hospital where I was doing my general training.

She was of small build, with a very determined chin and a strong Scottish accent, due to her having come from the Highlands of Scotland. She was several years older than most of us, and she told us that she was the eldest of six children. Her parents were very poor, and they had sacrificed a great deal to enable her to come to England to train as a Nurse. She was most conscientious and very intense but had no sense of humour. We laughed and joked about her, but really, we were all very fond of her.

Matron promised her she would arrange for her to have her holiday at the end of December so that she could be back in Scotland for the New Year.

Our Jane pinched and screwed and saved, and never spent a penny beyond church collections and postage stamps, and, of course, we all pulled her leg. One day she told me she had saved all the railway fare she needed to take her home for the great Scottish festival.

About a week before Christmas, however, a notice was pinned up in the Nurses' dining-room which read: 'Probationer X has lost her purse containing £200. If anybody finds it, will they please bring it to my office. Matron.'

The purse never turned up, and our Jane went about looking very sad. When we sympathized with her she muttered 'It's just one of life's little crosses; I must start saving all over again.'

Home Sister went to Matron and asked permission to collect some money for Jane to go home. Matron willingly agreed, and herself gave £5 to start the fund. We all gave what we could, and the money was quickly collected. On Christmas morning it was presented to Jane, but all she could say was, 'I thank you all, but I cannot say more, or I shall cry.' The tears were already rolling down her cheeks.

Our Jane had her holiday and thoroughly enjoyed herself. When she returned, however, the pinching and saving started all over again. Some months later, she went to Matron, and pushing a shabby old purse in front of her, just said 'I am returning the money you collected for me to go home.'

'I cannot accept it, Nurse,' said Matron. 'The money was given to you because the Nurses liked and respected you, and, in any case, many who contributed have left the hospital, having finished their training.'

'I thank you, Matron,' replied Jane. 'But my Scottish independence will not allow me to accept your charity. Use it for what you think best.'

When she had finished her training, our Jane joined a Presbyterian Mission and caught some rare Asiatic fever from which she never recovered. Dear old Jane. I hope one day I shall meet her in the great Beyond.

An Unknown Doctor

I once worked for a short time in a Nursing Home where we had a married woman help. She had a heart of gold but was very rough and ready, and would insist upon addressing everyone as 'my cock'.

Her husband, Bill, became ill and attended hospital as an out-patient. She returned one day exclaiming, 'Bill is going to see another Doctor on Wednesday.'

'Which one?' I asked.

'Doctor Barry Meal, my cock.'

'Don't be so silly, Mary,' I replied. 'There is no such person.

Barium meal is a treatment given to prove the process of digestion.'

She did not believe me until I rang through to the hospital and got them to explain the process to her.

The Mystery Baby

At the time of this incident, I was doing general district nursing and just relief midwifery.

One morning, whilst finishing my breakfast, I received an urgent call to visit Mrs. A. who lived near my lodging.

When I arrived I was let in by a cheery person who said, 'Good morning, Nurse, it is a lovely baby.' I told her she should have sent for Nurse Q, as I only did emergency baby work. 'Anyhow,' I said, 'now that I am here, I will go up and see Mrs. A.'

When I got upstairs, I found the said Mrs. A sitting up in bed nursing a bouncing baby with masses of ginger hair. 'Good morning, Nurse. Will you please see to my baby?' she asked.

'Yes,' I replied, 'what is wrong with it? It looks a very healthy child to me.'

The woman looked rather sheepish and said, 'I have just adopted it, Nurse, and it is ten days old.'

It presented the appearance of being at least three months old to me, and I looked the woman straight in the face and said, 'Now Mrs. A, it is no business of mine, but you know very well that that baby is about three months old. What are you up to?'

'Well, Nurse,' she said, 'it's like this. I cannot have any children of my own, so I have adopted this baby and am trying to pass it off as my own. I have been wearing padding of various sizes for several months, just to fool the neighbours. Will you come in every day for ten days or so, and bath it?'

To say I was astonished is to put it mildly, but I was very inexperienced in those days and said: 'I will do as you ask.'

When I was coming away finally she asked, 'Will you please notify the birth?'

'Certainly not,' I replied. 'There is a heavy penalty for false information, and don't you try to register it before legally adopting it.'

My landlady, whose name should have been Parker, missed very little in the district, and she was pleased to tell me the baby had arrived one night in a taxi.

I replied, 'Babies have often arrived unexpectedly.'

'Rubbish, Nurse,' she answered. 'I have never known a baby before to arrive in a cream silk gown and white shawl.'

What of it?

I had been trying to explain antibiotics to an old lady on my East End district, and gave penicillin as an example. I told her it was a special mould discovered by a Scotsman named Alexander Fleming. She listened intently for some time and then scornfully exclaimed: 'What of it? When we were kids and came home with cut knees, my mother always used to scrape the mould from a pot of jam and put on the wound.'

I wished the ground could have swallowed me

At the hospital where I trained, we had our own laundry and it was one of the jobs of junior Nurses to take soiled linen every night and put in the tank. It was intended, of course, only for white cotton goods. One day Matron put up a notice demanding all first and second year Nurses to assemble in the Recreation Room after prayers.

When the Nurses were all present, Matron walked in, dragging behind her a badly torn blanket.

'Perfectly disgraceful,' she said. 'Chewed to pieces by the machine. A dreadful waste of public money.' Then followed a homily on economy, and finally, 'Somebody was stupid enough to put a blanket in the tank. Who was it?'

A meek little voice said, 'I did, Matron,' but since she was only a very junior Nurse, she was let off lightly.

I was not at the meeting, since I was then in my third year.

I heard a graphic account of it, however, from those who were.

A few weeks later, the Nurses were busy getting up various entertainments to amuse the patients at Christmas. There were several tableaux, and one of these included a Matron. Matron had very kindly lent some of her own uniform for the purpose.

After one dress rehearsal, I chanced to pass, and happened to see Matron's attire on a chair. The temptation was too great for me. I put it on myself and, getting a blanket off my own bed, I walked around the Staff Nurses' corridor, taking the Matron off, and dragging the blanket. 'Chewed to pieces by machinery,' I kept chanting. I was soon joined by about twenty nurses, and the hilarious laughter, which grew in volume, soon brought the Home Sister to see what was happening. As soon as she spotted me she said, 'Come with me to Matron, at once, blanket and all.'

I shall never forget the look Matron gave me and then she said: 'If you behave like a fool, I shall treat you as one. You can spend the next six weeks doing junior Nurses' work in the Men's Medical Ward.' As most Nurses and ex-Nurses will know, this is one of the most thankless tasks for any Nurse.

Granny Keeps up her Reputation

I had a busy East End London district all through the war, and just loved it.

An old lady I was attending was nearly a hundred years old. She was a real marvel. She could read without glasses and was only slightly deaf. She lived with her married daughter, who never seemed to appreciate her. When I said to her once, 'She is really amazing,' the daughter just remarked with a sniff, 'She's all right, but she never keeps her promises.'

One day the old lady remarked to me, 'Next Friday, my dear, I shall be one hundred years old. I am having a party and a large cake with a hundred candles.'

'Congratulations, Gran dear,' I said. 'I shall certainly come to see that wonderful cake.'

The great day came and I went to the house as promised. I

was surprised to find all the blinds down, and silence everywhere.

I knocked, and the door was opened by a very indignant daughter exclaiming: 'She's done it again, Nurse! She passed away peacefully at five minutes to twelve!'

Sheep's Lungs

I had a very interesting experience once when I was nursing in a Welsh district. Two small children had become rather ill with pneumonia, following measles.

The Doctor called one morning whilst I was visiting and before I left, he said: 'I am not at all happy with the condition of these children, Nurse, and the baby (a boy who was only eleven months old) appears to have little chance of survival.'

I went back to my lodging feeling very sad. My landlady brought me my dinner and asked: 'How is the baby, Nurse?' I told her he was very ill, and that the Doctor held out little hope for him.

'That's what they said when my Tessa had pneumonia,' she said, 'but we soon cured her with sheep's lungs.'

'Sheep's lungs?' I exclaimed. 'What on earth can they do?'

'It's a common treatment in Wales,' she said.

Up I got. 'I don't want any dinner, thank you. Tell me, how do you use sheep's lungs?'

'You bandage each one on the soles of the feet,' she said, 'and leave them there for twelve hours.' I felt worse then, but worse still when she added, 'The lungs are all shrivelled up then, and give out a most offensive smell.'

I went to a butcher I knew and asked for two sheep's lungs. To my surprise, he took my request as a matter of course and said, 'Pneumonia, I suppose?' 'Yes,' I said, 'how much do I owe you?' He just waved me away and said, 'Good luck.'

I went to the house and told the child's mother what I had done. She seemed very pleased, and together we bandaged the lungs on the child's feet. I said I would come back as late as I could in the evening and see how he was getting on. I did this, and found him rather restive, but sleeping quietly. The following morning I was at the house again early, and was surprised to see a marked improvement. Apparently, the lungs had burst, and we had to open the windows wide to let out the very objectionable smell.

When the Doctor came, he was really amazed. 'Whatever has happened here, Nurse?' he asked. I dare not tell him what we had done, but merely replied, 'Children change so quickly, Doctor.'

I asked the mother not to give me away, since I knew I would be in trouble if the Doctors got to know that I had done something so unorthodox. I have, however, always had the greatest respect for sheep's lungs since this incident.

W. E. F.

A Questionnaire for Junior Nurses

Nurses should complete this form immediately after serving their first year in the wards. The object of this form is to enable Matron to see what progress you have made, and to assess your relationship with (*a*) other members of the staff, and (*b*) the patients. You must answer all questions as fully and frankly as you can, always trying to remember that Matron, herself, was once human.

1. Did you enter nursing
   (*a*) Because you felt you had to enter nursing, and regarded it as a vocation?
   (*b*) Because you looked on it as some kind of State-run marriage bureau, which might help you to find a husband easily?
   (*c*) For the money?
2. Do you regard your Staff Nurse as being
   (*a*) Keen and efficient?

(b) Kind but very exacting?

(c) Just an old bitch?

3. If Sister asks where you have been, do you reply

(a) 'To get your drink, Sister'?

(b) 'Down to the toilet, what do you think?'

(c) 'What the hell's it got to do with you?'

4. If Sister congratulates you on your work and tells you you are the best Nurse she has ever had, do you

(a) Think she has suddenly gone crackers?

(b) Wonder what sort of a job she is going to give you next?

(c) Just faint?

5. What is a bed-pan?

(a) Is it something used extensively in the kitchen?

(b) Is it an object to be kept under the bed?

(c) Is it a receptacle in which to serve soup to patients who are bed-ridden?

If it is none of these, please say exactly what you think it is, and explain its uses fully. You may include suitable line drawings here, if you think they help to explain your answer.

6. Is an enema

(a) A flower?

(b) Someone who dislikes you?

(c) A pleasant form of entertainment?

7. If you were to assist him, which kind of bath do you think a male patient would most prefer?

(a) An ordinary bath?

(b) A blanket bath?

(c) A bath bun?

8. If a good-looking young male patient asks you to kiss him, do you

(a) Tell him firmly to behave himself?

(b) Call for Sister?

(c) Oblige him, and ask for more?

9. If the temperature of a male patient seems to be rising when you are giving him the thermometer, and feeling his pulse, do you assume
   (a) That his general feverish condition is getting worse?
   (b) That the thermometer is not reading correctly?
   (c) That a rising temperature is due entirely to the fact that you are in close proximity with him and holding his hand?

10. If a handsome young Doctor shows signs of becoming interested in you, do you
   (a) Try to disregard him altogether?
   (b) Play it slow, and give the impression that you might or might not?
   (c) Whisper to him quietly, when the first convenient opportunity presents itself, 'Where, and at what time?'

11. If you were given a choice of menus for your evening meal, in the Staff Canteen, would you choose
   (a) Roast chicken and strawberry flan?
   (b) Fried fillet of plaice and chips, and lemon meringue pie?
   (c) The customary rissoles and rice?

12. If you go out on your first evening date, and return back very late, do you
   (a) Try to creep in very quietly, and go up to your room as noiselessly as possible?
   (b) Wake the other inmates of your room, and give them a lurid description of all the exciting things you have been doing?
   (c) Drop on your knees and ask to be forgiven?

Cyril Watts.

Some of My Favourites

Here are a few of the medical jokes I can remember, which have made me smile.

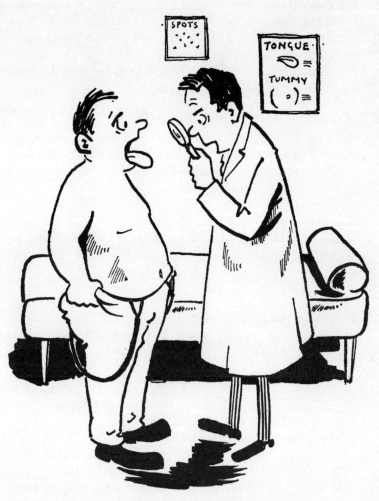

DOCTOR: 'Um . . . I shouldn't put it back: it might poison you.

A young man lay in a hospital bed with his head so obscured by heavy bandaging that only one eye and the crown of his head were visible. In an effort to cheer him up, a visiting clergyman greeted him humorously.

'Well, well, well,' said he jokingly, 'we are in a pickle aren't we? And what exactly is your trouble?'

The young man peered coldly at his visitor with his one available eye, and grunted, 'Dandruff!'

*   *   *

Said the Doctor's wife: 'A new cooker for my Christmas present? Thank you sweetheart. I'm very grateful. Now guess what I'm giving you for Christmas – a new stethoscope.'

*   *   *

Examiner: 'Who was Florence Nightingale?'

Trainee Nurse (hesitantly): 'Er . . . was she a girl who sang in Berkeley Square?'

*   *   *

A kipper walked into a Doctor's surgery and said: 'Is it true what I keep hearing about smoking being very bad for you?'

'Yes,' replied the Doctor, 'I'm afraid it has been proved true'.

'Funny,' said the kipper, 'smoking has completely cured me.'

*   *   *

The telephone rang at the hospital and the operator answered.

'Can you tell me, please, how Sid Sykes is?'

'Do you know which ward he is in?'

'Ward 12.'

'Wait a minute, I will put you through to the Sister.'

'Sid Sykes?' said the Sister. 'He seems to be getting on very nicely.'

'Has he had his operation yet?'

'Yes, he had it last Tuesday.'

'Was it successful?'

'Yes, the surgeon was very pleased with it.'

'Do you know when he will be having his stitches out?'

'In about a couple of days from now, I should think.'

'He won't be long before he comes out then, I expect?'

'Only two or three days probably. Can I tell him who rang, and is there any message?'

'Yes, this *is* Sid Sykes ringing from Ward 12. I just wondered how I was getting on. Nobody seems willing to tell you anything here.'

Joe (Mr. Piano) Henderson.

A Classic Escape

The story of Jake's famous escape from a mental ward has been told many times, and doubtless it will go down in history on a par with Anthony's escape from Cleopatra, or Hannibal's escape from the Alps, but the following account is thought to be authentic as it was recounted by a patient who had shared the same ward as Jake.

Jake was walking around one day, rubbing his hands and saying: 'I must escape, I must escape!'

The rubbing of his hands made a mass of sores, so he took one of these saws and cut a way through the bars of his window. Outside it was pouring with rain. The rain, in fact, was coming down in sheets, so he took a few of the sheets, tied them together, and used some of them to lower himself from the window. Down in the yard he found himself facing a high wall, but looking around, he discovered a piece of wood. With one of his saws he cut the piece of wood in halves. Two halves make a whole, so he crawled through the hole into the street beyond. By this time the rain had turned into snow and it made a thick blanket on the ground. He took up the blanket, wrapped himself up in it, and went to sleep.

On waking, he felt cold, and was a little hoarse, so without delay he mounted the horse and rode off down the street. Everywhere birds were singing, and bees came buzzing by, so he jumped on one of the buses and went to the top deck. He noticed the lady passenger in front of him had a ladder in her stocking, and as she went to get off the bus he climbed down the ladder and got into a taxi near by. He asked the taxi-man to drive him to Piccadilly Circus, where he met two tarts. He ate one of these, went home with the other, and has never been heard of since.

Anon.

Some of London's Hospitals

It may surprise many people to know that today there are over 300 hospitals in London, but I guess that many outside the profession will be more surprised to learn that two London hospitals – those of St. Bartholomew and St. Thomas – have been treating patients for over 800 years.

St. Bartholomew's Hospital – known everywhere affectionately as 'Barts' – is said to have been founded by a man who was a king's jester. Rahere was a jester at the court of Henry I, and on a visit to Rome he was taken ill. During this illness, he vowed to St. Bartholomew that if he got better, he would found a hospital for the poor in the saint's name. He did get well, and on returning to England, he persuaded the King to give him a piece of land on which to build his hospital. The King agreed, and with his own hands, and with the help of a few friends, Rahere built his hospital and continued to control it for twenty years.

None of the original building remains – it was rebuilt in 1552, again in 1729, and several new departments have been added to it since – but it still retains a legal document bearing Rahere's seal.

Throughout the ages, many famous names have been associated with the hospital, and one of its early benefactors was

Thomas à Becket, the renowned Archbishop of the 12th century. London's most famous chief citizen, Richard Whittington, was another.

Famous men who have served the hospital have included William Harvey, who discovered the circulation of the blood, and John Abernethy, who is still regarded as one of the greatest lecturers medicine has ever seen. It is said that this man lost a lucrative Royal appointment because he once refused to visit George IV until he had finished a lecture he was giving at the hospital.

St. Thomas's Hospital has had a varied career since it was first opened several hundred years ago and accommodated its first patients on rush beds laid out on the floor. Fire completely destroyed the first hospital, and during the Reformation the hospital on a new site was closed for twelve years. The closure was due to the fact that the hospital was associated with a saint, and efforts were made to get it re-opened under the title of 'The King's Hospital'. The people of London, however, strongly resented this change, and a way round this difficulty was eventually solved by finally convincing the public that the saint concerned was none other than St. Thomas the Apostle. This seemed to satisfy the mood of the time.

Dick Whittington, four times Mayor of London, was one of its early benefactors, and an old document states that 'noble marchaunt Rycharde Whytyndon, made a newe chambyr with viii beddys for young wemen that had done a-mysse in truste of a good mendement'.

The coming of the South-Eastern Railway to Charing Cross caused the hospital to be moved to Lambeth, but since the route went through the grounds of the old hospital, the railway paid nearly £300,000 by way of compensation.

A new hospital was opened later by Queen Victoria, and this included the Nightingale Home, which had been founded by Florence Nightingale from a gift of £50,000 which had been given to her to mark the value of her work in the Crimea. During the war, the hospital suffered badly, not only from high explosive bombs and flying bombs, but also from frequent attacks by incendiary bombs. It is interesting to note, however, that, despite these numerous bombings, not a single patient was killed, although fewer than eleven of the hospital staff lost their lives. This goes far, I think, to prove the devotion of doctors and nurses alike.

One of the more recent, but certainly one of the most loved hospitals in London, is the Great Ormond Street Hospital where the needs of sick children are catered for. Until the middle of last century, there was no special hospital in London to which children could go, and the majority of hospitals, in fact, definitely refused the admission of children on the grounds that they might easily introduce infection which could start up epidemics among the adult patients.

A story is told of these days of a newspaper seller who was shocked to see a small boy distorted from rickets, playing in the thick mud in the gutter. He asked the small child accompanying the boy, 'Does he ever see a Doctor?' 'Wot Doctor?' came the surprised reply, 'wot's the use when it's rickets? 'E'll 'ave to grow out of it. That's wot 'is young sister died of.'

In 1851 records were compiled which showed that 50,000 people died annually in London, and out of this total, 21,000 were children under the age of ten.

These figures alarmed a certain Dr. Charles West and he was also horrified by the sights he saw daily at a children's dispensary at which he worked. He gradually made up his mind that he would try to found a hospital to which none but young children should be admitted. Accordingly, in the spring of 1851 he walked the streets of London looking for a suitable place. Eventually he came to 49 Great Ormond Street, a fine old eighteenth-century mansion, which was deserted. Moreover, it was to let, and what was more important still, the rent asked for was low. He took his courage in both hands and hired it, and from these humble beginnings has come the great hospital of today, which is known and respected the world over. At the beginning, Queen Victoria – herself with a growing family – became its first patron and subscribed £100. At first there were only ten beds and a mere handful of out-patients. Many people were still suspicious of doctors, especially where children were concerned, but news of the hospital's good work quickly spread, and within less than five years, more than a thousand children had been inmates, and over thirty thousand had attended the out-patients' department. The old house has since been replaced by a splendid modern hospital.

One of the most interesting times in the hospital's varied career was when it was made known that Sir James Barrie bequeathed his *Peter Pan* play to the hospital, which meant that all future royalties from the play would go to swell the hospital's income. Since *Peter Pan* seems destined to go on for ever, this has meant a great deal. One wonders if Barrie's action sprang from an item which was found later in one of his notebooks. This read, 'Play. Boy who can't grow up. Runs away from pain and death.'

The present building was opened by the King and Queen in 1937, and from 1919 to 1921 the Princess Royal trained at the hospital as a Probationer.

The well-known Westminster Hospital grew out of the charity and vision of four men who met regularly at a coffee shop in Fleet Street. They based many of their talks on the Parable of the Good Samaritan, and the command 'Go and do thou likewise' first prompted them to distribute gifts among prisoners in the London gaols. Later they extended their activities to the poor and needy generally, and within a short time they also resolved to cope with the sick poor 'who were exposed to view on the streets and constituted an eye-sore'. Within a few years they were pledging their support and making plans to care for these people in an infirmary. They rented what was really the first Westminster Hospital at £22 a year, and with twelve beds, their original staff consisted of a Matron, a maid-servant, and a messenger.

During following years, the hospital was moved to different near-by sites, and many additions and alterations were carried out, until in 1939 the King and Queen opened what was then the most modern and best equipped hospital in London.

Westminster Hospital has always been in the forefront when new advances in medicine have been made, and millions of people all over the country have cause to thank the hospital for its pioneering spirit. One striking example of this is when the use of radium was just being realized, and the surgeons of Westminster Hospital asked for a supply of the precious substance. The request came when the Governors were just completing expenditure on another expensive project, but so eager has the hospital been to further any new treatment which seemed promising, that the Governors did not hesitate to raise £60,000 to buy the radium needed. Thus started the much-needed treatment which has since proved so valuable in cases of malignant disease.

Guy's Hospital is one of the few hospitals which takes its name from an actual person. Most others are named after a place, a district, a street, and so on. Guy's, however, has its name in memory of Thomas Guy a publisher and financier of Stuart times, who left sufficient money in his will for the hospital to be set up.

Talk of Guy's, and many people's thoughts immediately turn to rugby and to the thundering good rugger team which the hospital is always capable of turning out. This, of course, is due to the fact that, above everything else, Guy's is a teaching hospital, and always has a number of young students who have learnt their rugby the hard way in public schools and universities. Always in the wards there are groups of students studying patients with varying complaints in different beds. Always, too, there are groups of students watching operations in the operating theatre, and the more interesting operations are relayed to students outside the theatre on special television screens.

Dentistry forms an important part of the hospital's work, and an observer can see rows and rows of chairs with patients sitting in them, and students gazing intently into open mouths. There is also a constant drumming of drills as they are set to work on their several tasks. In another department students are shown how dentures should really fit and may themselves be trying to make a patient feel happy and comfortable with a new set of teeth.

One of the most interesting places at Guy's is the museum, which is famous all over the world. Most remarkable of all the exhibits, is the collection of wax models which were made by Joseph Towne. These models were made many years ago, but the secret of their modelling died with Towne, and no one has been able to make examples like them since. He reproduced horrifying human conditions in magnificently true colourings, and we are told that each model is anatomically perfect. In a special show-case is a model of a skeleton, accurate in every detail, which is said to have obtained for Towne his post at Guy's. Displayed alongside the skeleton are the instruments with which the artist is said to have carried out his work and, looking at them, one can but wonder how he ever managed to achieve his miraculous results.

A Consultant.

After an Operation

I'm so 'accident prone' that a friend used always to say to me '– and when he woke up in hospital'.

The last visit was not an accident. It was to have a neurofibrole and remove it from the thorakkers. Firstly they locate it and many an ex-rayle front side hip and how's yer father. 'Ah,' the surgeon said, showing me a large X-ray: 'That's it there,' and pointly fingold to a large lump well up in the chesky region. I vouchsafed that it seemed a bit near the vertebrale. 'Fp-t,' he ejaculated. 'Plenty of roomy for the knife'n slitty. Ten days, and you'll be out for convalessy.' So I went in.

Firstly there's the hypodermy injectoers with a rusty sawn-off shot gold; deep breathe it, and fade away to the far flummers. Then come the emerge into daylight. Large dangly bottle plasmold'n pipers feedy transfusion, and me all comftibold feeling as if on the other side of the fence and like it, but soon realized that it was the brave new whirl I was back to and somewhat disappointed.

Impressions: Deep joy in the hospitold, radiant favial of the Nurses, bread pan uncomfitbold, and no more worry about the knif'n poisy. Oh no.

Stanley Unwin.

Some Medical Tit-Bits

I have been in the hospital service for a long time and, over the years, I have picked up a lot of interesting stories and sayings, both from other members of the staff, and also from the patients who have been under my care. The following are a few, of many, which I can at present remember.

Some time ago we had a little Polish man in the Rehabilitation Ward. We were helping to get him walking after a long spell of arthritis. One day the Doctor asked, 'How long have you been in this country?'

'Two years,' said the patient.

'And what was your last job?'

'I don't know,' said the Pole, 'but it was hard work.'

*   *   *

A lady went to her Doctor and was advised to take a rest.

'But Doctor,' she said, 'you haven't looked at my tongue.'

'No need to,' was the reply. 'I'm sure that wants a rest too.'

*   *   *

A Sister went into her ward during the visiting hour and was surprised to see that one patient had a gas meter on his locker. She asked the visitor why it was there.

'Well,' said the visitor, 'you see he can't read books, he can only read a gas meter.'

$$* \qquad * \qquad *$$

There's no fun in medicine, but there's a lot of medicine in fun.

$$* \qquad * \qquad *$$

Two Doctors met in the street. 'Good morning,' said one, 'I see you're very well. How am I?'

$$* \qquad * \qquad *$$

An old man went to a Doctor and complained he was losing his hearing.

'How old are you?' asked the Doctor.

'Ninety-two,' was the reply.

'Ah,' said the Doctor, 'you've heard quite enough!'

$$* \qquad * \qquad *$$

Our Medical Superintendent went into a ward and saw a young Nurse rummaging through a drawer full of equipment.

'What are you looking for?' he asked.

'I don't know what it is,' she replied, 'but I shall recognize it when I see it.'

$$* \qquad * \qquad *$$

A lorry driver walked into a hospital Casualty Department, and the Sister in Charge asked him what he wanted.

'I've got gravel,' was the gruff reply.

The Sister gave him an injection, got him into pyjamas and dressing-gown, and took him to the Casualty Officer.

'You say you have gravel?' asked the Doctor.

'Yes,' was the brief reply. 'Three tons, on the lorry outside.'

$$* \qquad * \qquad *$$

An elderly man complained of a pain in his right leg.

'It's just old age,' said his Doctor.

'Can't be that,' said the patient, 'the other leg's the same age, and that don't ache!'

* * *

Examiner: 'Do you know what this bone is?'

Baffled examinee: 'No, do you?'

* * *

One of the Day Sisters finished writing her report and found there was still quite a space at the bottom of the page, so she followed her usual practice and drew a vertical line through it.

The Night Sister noticed this, and asked the junior Night Nurse if she knew why this was done.

The Nurse had no idea, but she felt she had to say something. 'Well,' she said, hesitantly, 'you have to draw the line somewhere don't you?'

* * *

An octogenarian decided it was high time that he derived some tangible form of benefit from our world famous National Health Service. So he went along to see his Doctor and demanded a chit, pro-forma, bill of lading, or what-have-you, authorizing him to draw a wig. The Doctor took a good look at his generous thatch.

'I'm sorry,' he said, 'but my professional opinion is that your condition does not warrant such an issue.'

Undismayed, the patient was ready with his alternatives. Spectacles, false teeth, surgical appliances, all in turn were hopefully requested, but all, alas, were sorrowfully refused.

'Well,' he said at last, 'what about one of those Duodenal Ulsters I've heard so much about?'

* * *

Questions put at a recent nursing examination produced the following replies:

The definition of air? What you walk on over the week-end.

What is an anti-toxin? Something injected into somebody for the purpose of preventing something.

What do you mean by astragalus? People who stray behind on a route march.

*　　*　　*

It is said there was once a Dentist who invented a machine for extracting teeth by remote control. A fine steel chain came down to the patient's mouth, and a cap at the end screwed on to the tooth. A lever regulated the pull, which could be varied from five pounds to five hundred. The Dentist tested it by retrieving instruments which his Nurse-Receptionist had dropped down the sink. Then he called for his first patient.

A man came in with a large lower molar.

'None of the Dentists in town can shift it,' he said proudly, 'it's the roots.'

Eagerly the inventor set to work. At a hundred pound pull the man felt nothing. At a hundred and fifty his jaw remained firm. At two hundred pounds his left foot rose from the ground. Hastily the Dentist reversed, and the foot dropped back.

'It's the roots all right,' he said. 'You'd better see a horticulturist.'

Next came an elderly lady. Her diagnosis was easy.

'Impacted wisdom tooth,' said the Dentist, and coupled her up.

He pulled the lever, gazing hopefully across to the chair. The needle spun as the pressure rose in the gauge. Then came a loud click. The Receptionist fainted. And well she might! The old lady's skeleton had jerked clean out of her body!

The Dentist apologized, but the patient only smiled, and said it might happen to anybody. She lived for many years after that, and was known as the 'Quivering Lady'. She was proud of her acquired immunity to dental cares, gingivitis, and Smith Peterson nails. She kept the skeleton on a clothes hanger behind the door, and when feeling more quivery than usual, she would study the joints and think of the arthritis she had missed.

But never again did the Dentist use his machine for treatment. He kept it solely for extracting fees from miserly patients while they were under an anaesthetic.

* * *

There's a home for weary Nurses
Above the bright blue sky
Where Matrons never wonder
And Sisters don't ask why.
They wake you every morning
With steaming cups of tea
And all the weary patients
Can rest eternally.

* * *

'And who be you,' St. Peter said, 'that I see standing here?'
'I was a hospital Nurse,' she said, 'for many a weary year!'
The gates of heaven opened wide as Peter rang the bell.
'Come right inside, my dear,' he said,
'You've had your share of ——'

J. R. B.

Where's the Change?

Lord Inman of Knaresborough was House Governor of Charing Cross Hospital for fifteen years and Chairman for another fifteen. It is not surprising, therefore, that during that time he amassed a number of really good stories connected with the hospital.

On one occasion, he has said, a cockney came into the hospital complaining of acute pain in his stomach. He was given a very careful examination, and finally, Sir Herbert Waterhouse

Senior Surgeon at the hospital, carried out an operation and was successful in removing a sixpenny piece from the patient's inside. The next day, when he went to see the patient, he took the coin to him and handed it to him saying: 'I thought you might like to keep this as a souvenir.'

'Only a tanner?' growled the cockney. 'It was half a quid I swallowed! What have you done with the rest of the money?'

A mother who was expecting another baby wanted her young son to understand something of what was happening, and to prepare him for the arrival of a new brother or sister. 'Now, John,' she had said, 'I want you to save all your pennies so that we can buy you a baby brother or sister.'

John did all he could, and religiously saved as much as possible each week from his pocket money, until one of his mates at school told him one day that they had a new baby brother *and* sister at home – meaning, of course, twins.

'Gosh,' said John, 'you must have had to save up a lot of pennies to get both.' The reply John got amazed him, and he rushed home to his mother saying, 'It's all a swiz having to save up to buy a baby. You can get one of each for *nothing* at the Charing Cross Hospital!'

Alan Walsh.

The Patient Who Inspired Me

On the whole, I have been very fortunate in my life about my health. It is true that eight years ago I had a coronary thrombosis, and my heart specialist said that I was very lucky to survive. He encouraged me by telling me that he would make my heart better than it had ever been before. And his promise came true. Indeed, the other day when I had a check-up with him, his report was that I was a hundred per cent fit again.

As I left his consulting-room, my mind floated back to the only other time when I have been really ill. It was at the end of

PATIENT: 'I'm so constipated, Doctor, I sometimes spend an hour or two in the toilet.
DOCTOR: 'Do you take anything?'
PATIENT: 'Oh, yes: I always take my knitting.'

the war, and I had had too many buffetings on the Russian run. The intensity of the cold in the end destroyed my physical resources, and I found myself for many months in hospital. When I re-emerged, my London doctor, still unsatisfied with my condition, sent me to a clinic in North Wales, for further tests and treatment. I was in a very melancholy frame of mind, and was quite certain that my life was over. I found it so difficult in peacetime, after those years at sea, to pick up the threads of my career.

I think all human beings go through these periods of utter negation but, fortunately for the great majority, the mood passes.

I shall be eternally grateful for the gesture that a fellow patient made towards me in that health clinic. It happened one morning when Sister, brusque, but with the wisdom of her calling, came into my room, and announced that there was a little old gentleman asking for me on the next corridor.

'He's a writer too, but he writes for the films, I think. No, I don't think he's met you, but when he heard you were here, he said he'd like to see you.'

'I don't want to see anyone,' I protested.

'Nonsense, it will do you good. Make you forget your own troubles. His are much worse than yours,' she added, in her dour, Scottish voice, as I turned my face away, and instinctively hid my nails beneath the sheets. They had rotted, and become to my aching eyes the symbol of the complete negation that had drained away my strength, my usual fount of vitality. But the summons came back, like an echo, the next day, and the next. *Mr. Mayer is asking for you. Mr. Mayer is asking for you.* Finally, I put on my dressing-gown and walked along the passage and up the stairs to the corridor where lay the more expensive rooms. Sulkily, I knocked.

My first glance registered a small, frail, Jack-in-the-box propped up in bed, his eyes on the door. Very brilliant eyes, the only brightness in the parchment skin that was the colour of his nightwear; above, a shock of thick grey hair. I remember thinking at once that this was how Christ might have looked, the pain and the forgiveness in His melting eyes, had He lived to be twice His age on earth. And then the stranger on the next corridor spoke. 'It was good of you to come and see me, my friend.'

Instantly, something within me responded. It was as though I had never heard those two last words given their true meaning before. I sat down beside him and found it easy to establish contact at once, though I knew nothing then of his accomplishments, how he had made cinematic history with his scenarios for those two early masterpieces, *Warning Shadows* and *The Cabinet of Dr. Caligari*, in the days before the persecution of his people had become Nazi priority number one and Carl Mayer had fled into exile.

It was sad to watch the way his head jerked sideways on the pillow, his hands could not keep still, plucking at his stomach, like a supplicant, now sighing, now a sudden awful groan. I did not want to let my eyes stray from him again, because, beyond his bed, in this corner room, with windows on both sides, I could see into the garden where, in great waves, the daffodils were trumpeting their brief life across the grasss. The trees were in bud, and there was a sense of renewal and promise, remote from my own mood of incarceration. Moreover, the sun was so strong, flooding the room – I was not used to windows like this – that it pricked my eyes with tears. Or was it the contrast of that ashen face upon the pillows, and all the colour outside, the singing and the gold?

'My friend, you will come and see me again,' he whispered, as quite suddenly a spasm took hold of him, and he started ringing frantically for the nurse. 'An injection please.' His eyes were enormous, burning. '*Please.*' There was something terrible about the little tableau; the nurse, so clean and hygienic, suggested the implacability of death. I fled, as though from an appointment in Samara. Yet, as I retraced my steps to my own small room, with its restricted view, I was looking outwards once more; instead of myself, I was thinking of the man who at sight had called me his friend, and so without recognizing the moment, my own healing began.

Each day as I now grew stronger, I became tragically aware that in direct ratio to the new strength flowing through me, his own limbs were wasting away. On one occasion, against the direct advice of his Nurses, or, perhaps behind their back, he had got up, dressed himself somehow in his rather formal old-fashioned clothes, and leaning heavily on his ebony stick, he had jerked his way, like a marionette, to the little Welsh village that lay at the bottom of the drive.

I only heard afterwards of his brief escape. That afternoon, as I went to pay my customary call, he was smiling with delight, a child. 'Come in, my friend, come in. I have something for you.'

There beside him on his bedside table was a cup and saucer. He had discovered it in the local junk shop, the only one left of a set of exquisite Worcester. He touched it lovingly, caressing the pattern with his long, frail fingers. 'What beautiful things man can make,' he said.

I was to remember that image, when later, I pieced together fragments of Carl's story, learning how he had been discovered in one of the tube shelters by chance one night, at the height of the blitz, emaciated, sick, existing on cups of tea from a W.V.S. mug. And all because he possessed the soul of a true artist. (The phrase has a meaning after all.) For I discovered too, that after it had become imperative for him to escape from Germany, to sacrifice the great position he had built up in the Ufa Studios, and start all over again elsewhere, a wandering Jew, Hollywood had made him a series of ascending offers, but he had stubbornly refused them all, fearful lest he should be corrupted, his work altered, his advice ignored. Then came the war, and for a time film-making in England, except for propaganda, was at a standstill; in the chaos of the blitz, Carl Mayer became one of the multitude that nightly, as the light began to fade from the sky, burrowed underground.

From this obscurity they lifted him up again. That fantastic

71

character, 'Del', then head of Two Cities, one of the Rank group, made Carl his personal assistant and adviser, upon his own terms. (Not financial, but spiritual, the safeguarding of his artistic integrity, that meant everything to him.) 'My dear friend, it was wonderful to be at work again, under such conditions. I was so happy, I could not understand why I did not grow strong. Then the pain started, here in my side. I could not eat. In the middle of a script conference, I would be sick. They sent me to doctors, two, three, four doctors; they sent me to hospital. Finally, I came here. Del, he is paying for everything, has been so good to me. You see what a fine room I have, and I have promised to get well. There is so little time . . .'

'So little time . . .' I repeated. Already the daffodils were nearly over, soon the tulips would take their place, and then the roses.

'Yes, we were behind our schedule. I try to work on the script that must be finished. And you will help me, my friend. You must be very kind and help me.'

I mistook his gesture for pity. In his capacity for understanding, of which I was made more conscious every day, he was seeking to start me back along the road. For I believed myself to be washed up. Had I not broken down and confessed that I could no longer put two words together to make sense?

'How can I help you?' I protested wearily. 'I know nothing about script writing, though I should love to learn. But not at your expense, Carl. I can't see Two Cities giving me a job when I come out of prison.'

'But my friend, this is a sea story, and you were at sea, and I was not. It is the script that Leslie Howard was planning just before they shot down his plane. Now we must finish it, as best we can. The heroine is a merchant ship, a Liberty ship in a convoy to Russia. Is that not, as you say, your cup of tea?'

'I don't want ever to think about the sea again,' I burst out.

'But your eyes are as blue as the sea today. That means you are getting better, my friend.'

He had a directness, a kind of purity of approach, such as St. Francis of Assisi must have possessed talking to his birds. In that case, why did I not take seriously the prospects that he held out to me so generously? I suppose that my excuse would be that in the film world many extravagant promises are made; again, a clinic is like a religious community; you pour yourself out in the confessional, and then you return to the outside world and forget those long weeks of solitariness, their loyalties, and their sudden devotion.

I was convalescing in Sussex when the telegram came. I have it still. 'TWO CITIES WISH TO GET IN TOUCH WITH YOU. PLEASE COMMUNICATE WITH ME.' Then the number in Hanover Square, and the signature. I hastened there next day. He was lying in a darkened room, so that after the brilliance of the June light outside, it was difficult at first to distinguish his face from the pillow, while there seemed to be too great a mound of bed clothes weighing down his shrivelled body as I remembered it. And then he explained that his stomach had swollen right out, like a gourd. There was to be an exploratory operation in yet another nursing home, the next day. The clinic could do no more. I think he must have known his body was past treatment, even though the brilliance of his eyes seemed greater than ever.

'My friend, you see, I kept my promise. Always believe in people. It is the best way. Sometimes you will be disappointed, but more often, not. Life has been very good to me. Always when things were bad, something happened to make me believe again in the bounty of the world. So it will be for you, too, my friend.'

There was nothing that I could add. Instead, I thought how from that day until my own death, whenever anyone spoke of a man going to his destiny, and was it not all fated, the chance encounters at the crossroads, the good fortune and the bad, I would be walking down a long corridor again in a dressing-gown, and knocking, under protest, without a clue, upon an unknown door. I wanted desperately to thank him for all that he had done to give me back my confidence, but the words would not come. If only I could pump into his veins some of the health of mind and body that he had restored to me. If . . . and then the Nurse came back into the room and lifted him up in bed, like a baby, and at once I saw how he had diminished, even in the gap of weeks. She had her hypodermic syringe ready. Immediately the pain must have lessened, for he smiled as I went away, a tender, radiant smile. 'Nothing happens without a reason,' he said. 'Good-bye, my friend.'

Mercifully his spirit slipped away under the anaesthetic, for it was established that he had been suffering from an incurable disease, and had been suffering the most torturing agony that any human being can be expected to endure. Yet I had never heard him complain once, or rail against his God. And a few days later his reassuring presence was still with me in the room. I could see him once more putting out his hand to caress the Worcester cup and saucer, even as I put out my hand to sign the contract in the film office that was to mean for me the beginning of a new career.

Godfrey Winn.

Training School Howlers

On Domestic Ward Routine
'Fill a bowel of disinfectant and go all over the bed.'
'Scrape fluff off bottom so that the mattress will not rust.'
'Put mattress on bed then slip into a clean cover.'

Personal Hygiene
'A bath or thorough brushing will make the skin breathe.'
'The Great Plague started beneath the arms and spread all over Europe.'

First Aid
  'Muscle contraption is a cause of fractures.'
  'Muscles are capable of abominable reactions.'

Bathing in bed
  'Wash the chest and bust.'

Relieving Retention
  'Pour water over the gentiles.'

On Hospital Food
  'Four meals every four hours – everything in moderation!'
  'All food should be raped.'

Physiology
  'The bladder is lined with translated tissue.'
  'A tissue is a number of cells – all with the same ideas!'
  'The spines of the vertebrae are bifted!'
  'There are pediculi on each vertebrae.'

Various
  (After visiting a dairy.) 'At the milk dairy everybody is washed and inspected for cracks.'
  'The portal vein collects blood rich in nourishment from stomach and utensils!'
  'The Plenum System means as much air as possible entering with as little noise as possible.'
  'Quarantine is a period when people with infection should be insulated.'
  'Deffervescence is the time when all symptoms start to recline.'
  'Vitamin "E" is an anti-absorptive for the preservation of miscarriage.'
  'Pregnancy is brought about by its presence, abortion by its absence, therefore we must educate all expectant mothers.'
Miss D. M. Price, Principal Tutor, Bedford General Hospital Training School.

Together on Holiday

A small boy in a children's ward was being given a dressing by Nurse as the Matron looked on. Suddenly he turned to Nurse and said:

'Did you enjoy your holiday, Nurse?'

'My holiday?' asked Nurse. 'What do you mean? I haven't been away yet.'

'Oh,' said the boy. 'I thought you had, because I heard Doctor say that you and Matron had been at loggerheads for the past fortnight.'

Barbara Law.

An Undignified Entrance

My earliest appearances as an 'entertainer' were in the Military Hospital during the 1914–18 War. I was a boy soprano singing 'Roses of Picardy' in a bum . . . sorry, back-freezer, and if the concerts were in the evenings, I was excused homework. If they were in the afternoons, I was excused school and wired into the buns, cakes, and tea after the show. Then – horror of horrors – my voice broke! No more excused school and homework they said. But I was crafty – I bought two comic songs (having always been the school and choir comical codger) and started out as a comedian. I was naturally a little afraid of not getting laughs on my first appearance as 'A. Askey – Entertainer' – but I need not have worried. The ward floor was, as usual, very highly polished – I made my entrance, fell flat on my back, and came round with the Matron's assurance that I got the biggest laugh of the night!

You may remember we had another war about twenty years later, and by this time, my visits to the Army, Navy, and R.A.F. hospitals were much sought after. And what a success I was – until I visited a hospital at Aldershot one night. I thought my entrance was received with modified rapture but I thought 'I'll soon get 'em – perhaps they're very ill,' though they didn't look too bad. It was only when I came off to the sound of my own feet that they told me that the audience were French Canadians!

One of my earliest 'hospital' jokes in pantomime was, 'Here's a picture of me taken in hospital – I'm in the end bed.' Straight man: 'But the end bed's empty.' Me: 'Is it? – I must have got out for a minute!' But now the hospital jokes are not nearly as corny. There's the one about the Doctor who asked his lady patient if she . . . ooh! I can't tell you that one. But there's the one about the new Nurse who was asked to prepare a young man for . . . that's a bit tropical too. I know – there was the young student who was asked to remove the patient's spectacles and when the surgeon came . . . that's plain filthy!

Arthur Askey.

A Broody Hen

When I was in hospital on one occasion, a patient in a near-by bed called one morning for a Nurse and asked if she would kindly bring him a bed-pan. The Nurse fetched him the necessary article, made him comfortable, and then went on again with her various duties. She must have forgotten him since it wa. more than an hour later when she returned and asked him cheerily, 'Well, Mr. Briars, have you finished yet?' 'Finished!' shrieked the patient, angrily. 'I should think the blooming thing is hatching out by now.'

F. Favell.

Elizabeth Blackwell

I could describe many interesting incidents, some of them very funny, which have come to my notice, at one time or another, in various hospitals but, being a female, I think I would prefer, if I am capable of doing justice to the subject, to tell the story of the first woman who succeeded in storming the strong male barricade which had surrounded the medical field so tightly up to the middle of the last century.

The name of this important female was Elizabeth Blackwell, a young lady who came from Philadelphia. She was by no means a 'blue-stocking' but, on the contrary, her very attractive appearance, fine body lines, and mass of blonde curls, were capable – though not by intention – of turning the hearts and heads of any body of young men. Her determined chin, however, was evidence of the fact that she had a very strong will, and was prepared to do anything to achieve an ambition. She hated being with people who were sick, shrank away from the sight of blood, and turned pale when anyone spoke of dissection. She kept feeling strongly, however, that God was directing her, and that her sole mission in life was to become a Doctor. She tried to gain entry into twelve medical schools but was bluntly refused on every occasion. Still she went on trying, and eventually the break came.

One day in 1847, Dr. Charles A. Lee, Dean of the Faculty of Geneva Medical College in Western New York, rose timidly in front of the 150 young medical students in his class and began to address them.

'Young gentlemen,' he said, not without some little agitation, 'this College is faced with a situation unprecedented in the history of American medicine. A female, a young lady from Philadelphia, has requested admission to the medical school.

'This young lady – hum – has been highly recommended,' he continued, 'by an eminent Philadelphia physician. She has been refused admission by several larger colleges but – hum – felt that a "country" college would be freer from prejudice. Realizing the disturbing effect of a member of the other sex in your midst, the faculty is leaving it up to the class to decide. If a single student objects to her admission, a negative reply will be returned.'

The Dean's unusual speech stunned the medical students and,

talking among themselves, they decided that it could only be a hoax, perpetrated by the students of a rival school. They decided, however, to debate the question of her admission at a special meeting they arranged to be held in the evening. Every one of the 150 students attended this meeting, and student after student rose to make extravagant speeches in favour of admitting this unknown girl to their class. When the vote was finally taken, there was just one solitary dissenter and the rest of the class fell on him and mobbed him until he was eventually persuaded to agree. An imposing resolution was then announced pledging the young lady full support and adding, 'that no conduct of ours shall cause her to regret her attendance at this Institution'.

A letter was sent off to Elizabeth giving her the good news, but the writer was careful to point out that 'some may deem it bold in the present state of society'. Thus, from a meeting of students gathered together more in the form of a joke than anything else, came this very first entry of a woman into a medical college.

Once in, Elizabeth determined that, by careful study and conscientious working, she would prove that her acceptance had been worth while, and give a boost to the claims of intelligent and forward-looking females everywhere. Her great moment of triumph came on a day in January 1849 when she graduated and heard herself described as the honour-student of the year, having gained more marks in her examination than any of her colleagues.

Despite her very attractive appearance and the secret fear of the tutors that a woman in a male college might have a disastrous effect on the men students, nothing of the kind happened. Elizabeth's approach to romance was very matter-of-fact, and she wrote in her diary of keeping two eligible young males 'at a respectable distance, which I am quite capable of doing'. In another entry she speaks of her determination to become a physician and describes this as 'a strong barrier between me and all ordinary marriage'.

Contrary to what some had feared, her 'firm and determined

79

expression of face' soon caused a change of behaviour for the good among her male contemporaries. According to one account, her effect upon the usually 'rude, boisterous, and riotous' students, could only be described as miraculous. One asserts that 'for the first time a lecture was given without the slightest interruption', and that the 'sudden transformation of this class from a band of lawless desperadoes to gentlemen, by the mere presence of a lady, proved to be permanent in its effects'.

Her stay at the college was quite happy, and she made many friends. In the eyes of the townsfolk outside, however, she was regarded as someone to be despised. Whoever thought of a lady Doctor! She must either be a bad woman having evil designs on men, or just a plain lunatic. The ladies of the town would have nothing to do with her and effectively snubbed her, daintily lifting their skirts as she passed, so that she would not contaminate them.

In the college itself, Elizabeth was lucky to have as her particular guardian angel, the plump little Dr. Webster, who was the Professor of Anatomy. She describes him as 'a fat little fairy of a man, blunt in manner, and very voluble'.

It was in connection with one of Dr. Webster's classes that she faced her first real crisis. The Professor had come to a part in his talk which he felt sure must prove very embarrassing to Elizabeth if she were to listen to it. Moreover, he was in the habit of slipping in little stories and anecdotes of a kind which were accepted with glee by the male students but which would surely cause embarrassment to a woman – especially in those days.

He told Elizabeth of his difficulty frankly, advising her to keep away from the class, and offering to make up for this by promising to provide her with abundant opportunities for private tuition. She told the Professor she fully realized his predicament but added that she was particularly anxious to attend the lecture. She wrote him a letter to this effect and added that, if it would cause him less embarrassment, she would be quite willing to take her seat somewhere at the back of the class. Dr. Webster read her

'25 swabs, 18 clamps, 3 scalpels . . . we seem to be one keeper short!'

letter to the students and they immediately voted that she should be admitted and allowed to sit in her usual place. Elizabeth attended the lecture and was greeted by a great ovation from the rest of the students. She tells in her journal that the ordeal 'shocked her delicacy' but adds that she tried to keep from smiling, as those around her were doing, and maintained 'a grave indifference'.

Now that she had obtained her degree, and her first big difficulty was over, her real struggle began. Her ambition now was to be a surgeon but, despite her qualifications, there was not a hospital in America that would admit her. A friend suggested she should go to Paris, but although she set off hopefully, she was soon to suffer a severe disappointment when she found that the French Doctors were not even willing to recognize her degree. One after another advised her that all she could hope to do was to enrol at La Maternite as a student midwife.

In desperation she finally did just this but found life extremely hard. She often spent sixteen hours or more a day in heartbreaking and backbreaking drudgery but, although a scintillating and carefree-looking Paris lay just over the walls, she was allowed only once in her six months' stay to go outside the grounds of La Maternité.

One bright spot here, however, was that she did meet romance in the form of a handsome young intern named Dr. Hippolyte Blot. There is no doubt that the two really fell in love with each other, but Elizabeth still felt, deep down, that she had been singled out by God to open up medical careers for women. At the time she courageously wrote in her diary, 'Because of the stern life I have chosen, all thoughts of love and marriage must be put aside.' That she never forgot the young intern is evident from the fact that she was still writing about him wistfully more than forty years later.

From Paris she returned to America, hoping that, by now, she might be able to set up a private practice. More disappointments followed, since she could find no landlady who would allow her to put up a nameplate on the doorway. 'If I let a female Doctor's plate be shown,' said one, 'a mob might soon come and wreck the place.'

Finding no one who would take her, Elizabeth set out to borrow money and buy a house of her own. Patients did not come, and she spent the time studying the young girls all around her. She observed what effects the heavy clothing they wore had on their exercise, and the difficulty the body had to breathe, especially in their tightly laced corsets, and she also noticed what simple and often inadequate meals many of them took in an effort to retain a dainty figure. The more she thought about it, the more convinced she became that these conditions might be in some way responsible for the tuberculosis which was so rampant at this time.

Thinking on these lines caused an important change to come about in Elizabeth's career. She carefully prepared lectures on the subject, and she was successful in getting a group of Quaker women to listen to her lectures. So impressed were the women that they got together to provide a dispensary, in one of the poorest districts of New York, and asked Elizabeth to take charge of it.

Soon she had not too few patients but too many, and although the medical profession in general still refused to have anything to do with her, the work she was doing soon became more widely known and was appreciated by those who had vision. As she worked in isolation she planned for the day when she could establish the first hospital in the world to be staffed entirely by women Doctors. This, she felt, was the only way in which women who thought as she did would be able to obtain the experience and practical tuition they so badly needed.

For six years she kept her dream alive and kept planning all the time for the new hospital which she felt sure she would be able to establish. All the time more and more people were beginning to take notice of her and listened to her pleadings. The *New York Herald* sent a reporter to interview her, and published a long article describing her work. Next, a famous Doctor spoke approvingly of what she was doing and, finally, Henry Ward Beecher launched a fund which raised more than ten million dollars and enabled her to open the doors of the New York Infirmary for Women and Children in 1857.

Elizabeth now turned her attentions mainly to hygiene. She was convinced that sunlight, fresh air, clean and wholesome food, and particularly pure water, would do much to prevent diseases which customarily led to harsh treatment by the doctors who were dealing with them. She made her own hospital, for those days, a model of cleanliness and brightness. 'Ugly, dirty surroundings dishearten people,' she once wrote, 'make it harder for them to get well.' She allowed her students to serve in the wards, and always insisted upon all the members of her staff being immaculately turned out.

Soon her fame, and the condition of her hospital, was spreading all over the world. First came an emissary from the Czar to examine her hospital and methods, since twenty-five ladies were seeking admission to the medical schools of St. Petersburg. Then came a query from Sweden where fifteen young women were anxious to study medicine in Stockholm. Gradually the gates of medicine were opening out to women in all parts of the world, and Elizabeth saw her fondest dreams coming true. News came that the first woman student had entered a medical college in Algiers, and she herself, appointed the first American Negro woman to receive a medical degree, as a member of her staff.

Despite all this progress in many parts of the world, the struggle in England was still very bitter, and Elizabeth was invited to come to the aid of women in this country who wanted to make a career out of medicine. Shortly after she arrived over here, seven young women dared to enrol in the medical department of the University of Edinburgh, but the Press immediately labelled them as 'the shameless seven', and they were mobbed by male students and pelted with mud. An investigation followed, and the seven girls were promptly expelled.

'Start a medical college of your own,' retorted Elizabeth. Not only did she give the advice, however, but she made strenuous efforts to raise the funds necessary to open the London School of Medicine for Women.

Advancing years and illness were now beginning to take their toll, but Elizabeth's fervour remained unabated. With her fixed ideas on the prevention of illness, she founded the National Health Society, with the motto 'Prevention is better than cure', and delivered a series of lectures to working people throughout London.

One other thing for which she is remembered is that she was the first person of any standing to write a pamphlet on sex instruction. She was prompted to do this by the misery she had seen among Victorian brides, caused by sex ignorance. She tried no less than twelve publishers to print her pamphlet but all looked at it with horror. Not to be outdone, she finally printed it at her own expense, and saw it achieve a wide circulation.

As she grew older, she could do little practical work herself, but she continued almost to the end, to work in her study and answer the correspondence and queries which kept flooding in from all parts of the globe.

She was still displaying clear intellectual gifts when she finally died at the age of eighty-nine in 1910, and one of her admirers wrote: 'She lived to see the river of her individiaul life expand into the ocean of a world movement.'

Janet Gould.

He Couldn't Find It

The following happened during one of my spells of night duty.

A patient aged about sixty-five to seventy had had an amputation of one leg. He was perfectly O.K. during the daytime but at night he frequently became a little confused, and would frequently attempt to get out of bed. Each night, we took the usual precautions of putting chains around the bed so that we could hear the first noise and rush to prevent him.

On this particular night, we were all extremely busy dealing with a patient in a side ward, and when I at length dashed out of the side ward to check on the old man, I found he had already succeeded in getting out of his bed. I was just in time to see him standing on one leg and looking down at his empty pyjama leg with a puzzled expression. Then I heard him suddenly exclaim, 'Where's the other b—— got to?'

Mary C. Berry, S.C.M., S.R.M., M.S.R.

Form for Nocturnal Workers

A copy of Form ND/1 which has been drawn up with a view to encouraging nurses to prefer night duty. A careful study of it should do much to alleviate the present shortage of nurses.

1. On which particular ward would you prefer to work?

2. Which nights off do you require?

3. Do you desire a different set of nights off each week?

4. If answer to the above is 'yes', please let the Night Sister know when you intend taking them, giving at least twelve hours notice.

5. Do you think one hour is enough for the main night meal?

6. Should you wish to take longer, will you let your relief know.

7. Do you want a partner of the same or opposite sex?

8. If answer to number 7 is 'opposite', please state age and type.

9. Detailed description of the above may be given, if not embarrassing.

10. What type of armchair do you prefer?

11. Do you wish Night Sister to do her rounds
    (a) regularly?
    (b) irregularly?
    (c) when asked?
    (d) not at all?
12. Do you really want to go on night duty? If so, give reasons
    on separate sheet of foolscap or roll of wall paper.

J. B.

Memories of a Country Doctor

Doctoring has been in my family for generations, and my maternal great-grandfather, grandfather, uncle, and myself, have all practised medicine at Bideford. I am now retired after having served the people of that area for over fifty years, but the tradition is still being carried on by my elder son who is a Doctor in the service of British Petroleum in Aden.

I have no personal recollections of the first two generations, but there is a family relic of my grandfather in the shape of an ebony-handled surgical instrument known as a 'perforator'. This was used in cases of difficult child-birth to reduce the unborn child's head to manageable proportions. The eleven notches borne by the ebony show that it had been regularly employed and, presumably, frequently to good effect.

Practice conditions in my early days were markedly different from those of the present time, and not always to the advantage of the Doctor. One was very much 'out on a limb', and specialists, as we know them today, had not been born. It can truly be said that, in the old days of the family Doctor, a person was usually treated solely by him from the womb to the tomb.

I have naturally had many interesting and unusual incidents in my experience, and here are two or three examples which show how odd such experiences could be.

I was called from my warm bed one wet and windy night, to the house of the widow of an army officer four miles away. On entering her very cosy bedroom, I found her sitting up in bed. She was reading a book and seemed to be very much in her usual good health. On inquiring what was the matter, she replied brightly, 'Doctor, I am so sorry to bother you, but I woke up suddenly remembering that I had not got anybody to sign my pension form.' I signed it for her, but not too cheerfully, and I can still remember her puzzled expression as she tried to grasp what all the fuss was about.

In the early nineteen-twenties, a dear old lady owned a fine middle-aged blue and yellow macaw called Chockie, to which both she and I were devoted. She sent one day in great distress, with the message that Chockie could not stand on his perch. When I arrived, he was lying on his back on the bottom of the cage and, to my inexperienced eyes, he seemed in every sense to be on his last legs. 'Can't you do anything for him, please?' I had vague recollections of reading somewhere about experiments on feeding pigeons on unpolished rice, so producing loss of balance. As a shot in the dark, I prescribed Bemax three times a day, and went sadly away. When the owner died some years later, Chockie was in his prime, in spite of the difficulties of getting his favourite tropical seeds during the time of the Second World War. He was finally transferred to Bristol Zoo, where I am certain I recognized him many years afterwards.

One very hot summer day, a call came to visit a house built on the end of a pebble beach. As I approached, I was conscious of an indefinable, but disagreeable, aura. The door was opened to me by Her Grace herself, and without a word, she led me to a bedroom, flung open the shutters, and pointing a dramatic finger, cried: 'Look'. The vision was more than matched by the smell. Under the window-sill lay the highly decomposed body of an enormous whale. 'Well,' she said, 'what are you going to do about it?' After a moment to get my breath, I replied, 'Duchess, this is a job for the Medical Officer of Health.' At first this official did not share my sense of urgency, but ultimately arrangements were made to cut up the corpse, the portions being dragged by hook and chain to a distant sandhill. But even this was not the end, for every dog followed the trail, bringing back the choicest morsel to lay on his master's hearth rug.

At the beginning of my career, I was awakened by a farmer ringing my night-bell, for telephones were rare luxuries in those days. His wife urgently needed me for the birth of her first baby. At that time, midwifery always filled me with apprehension, and even my limited experience had told me that this particular case was going to be an anxious business. My fears were confirmed when I arrived at the distant farm to face complications with which I was not too familiar. After taking off my coat and grappling for a long time with a difficult instrumental delivery, I wiped my streaming brow and put on my coat again. Dawn was breaking as I left the house. In the semi-darkness I saw the husband emerging from a building at the rear of the farm. 'Ah, Doctor,' he said, 'you are just the man I was looking for. Would you mind taking off your coat and lending me a hand.' I returned with him to the building, and by the light of a hurricane-lamp, I saw a calf's head protruding, with a rope around its horns. 'Now, Doctor, just take hold of that rope, put your foot against the stall and *pull.*' I pulled, but for a very long time nothing happened. Then, with a pop like that of a giant champagne cork, the happy event occurred. For the second time I put on my coat. The farmer accompanied me to the gate on the road, thanking me warmly for assisting him. Then he had a sudden thought. 'By the way,' he said, 'how's the wife?'

Once upon a time, three spinsters lived together in a large house. And this is not a fairy story. Let them be called Louisa, Anne, and Charlotte. Louisa, the eldest, had spent fifteen years in bed, for no discernible reason. As this state of affairs had gone on so long, the family thought it necessary to call in a specialist. The physician, with a special interest in diseases of the heart, duly arrived. To my utter astonishment, he took the gravest view of her case, bluntly telling the sisters that she had no more than three months to live. The specialist himself died – strangely of heart trouble – some months later, but for a year or two there was no noticeable change in Louisa's condition. Then, one day, I received an urgent call to visit her. To me she seemed very much as usual, so I took the sisters into an adjoining room to try to clarify the position. 'She wants to get up,' said Charlotte. 'And why ever not?' I asked. 'Oh, Doctor, you don't under-stand. You remember that the specialist told us she had only three months to live?' 'And do you remember that I told you that I did not believe him?' I replied. With natural reluctance they finally came to the root of the matter. 'We have been using up all her clothes,' said one, 'and now she has only her nighties to wear.' I offered to accompany them whilst this dis-tressing news was broken to the patient. Louisa became a little pale, and turned her face to the wall without comment. Some ten years later, she died – but not of heart disease.

Dr. Martin Littlewood, (Retired G.P.)

Some Medical Jokes

I have heard a number of medical jokes which have made me smile from time to time, and here are just a few I can remember at the moment.

A workman had a picture he wanted framed, and he asked one of his friends in the factory if he could make him a suitable frame for it.

'Certainly,' said his friend, 'what size frame do you require?'

'Three square foot,' came the reply. The friend did not like to show his ignorance, and a little later he went to the Shop Steward and asked, 'Here, Harry, what's a square foot?'

'I don't rightly know,' replied Harry hesitantly, 'but if you like to go along to the Doctor and get a paper, I'll see that you're soon in benefit.'

*   *   *

You may have heard of the young man who had an X-ray photograph taken of himself because he couldn't think what so many girls saw in him.

*   *   *

The janitor had been at his Yorkshire hospital for more than half a century. His reminiscences were being sought, and the question was put to him as to the changes he had seen during these many years. He thought deeply before replying: 'Well, if you had been standing where you are standing now twenty-five years ago, you'd be on a mortuary slab!'

*   *   *

A countryman who was very deaf visited the market in the near-by town one day, and noticed somebody selling guaranteed hearing aids. Since these were priced at only five pounds each, he bought one, but was annoyed when he opened the packet and found only a piece of string knotted at both ends. He returned to the salesman and became very cross, whereupon he was informed that he had only to place one knot in his ear and the other knot in his waistcoat pocket, and everyone he spoke to would be certain to shout back like blazes!

Joe Loss.

Not Fit for a Dog

I have come across many out of the ordinary incidents during my work as a Nurse. Here are just two or three examples of what I mean.

One very wild night, a Doctor was called to a lonely farm among the fells. He had to come a distance of six miles from the market town in order to get there, and his journey had been anything but pleasant. The District Nurse lived in the village less than a mile from the farm. When the Doctor arrived and examined the patient, he could find very little the matter with him. Feeling rather cross, he said, 'I do wish you had sent for the Nurse and asked for her opinion before making me come all these miles at a time like this.' 'What!' exclaimed the patient's wife, 'send for the Nurse? You couldn't expect a dog to come out on a night like this!'

A patient, living in an isolated farmhouse, was really a very likeable old lady, always with a twinkle in her eye. For all that, however, she was often a bit difficult and a little obstinate. I used to visit her each morning and every day she would remark, 'Why do you come at night? I wish you would come in the morning when it is light.' One day, rather exasperated, I replied 'Look out of the window Mrs. —— it's a glorious light sunny morning. How can you think it's night?' Came the quick retort, 'You're drunk, Nurse!'

I was visiting a fellside farm where the old farmer was extremely proud of his fell pony. Wishing to please the old man, I asked to see the pony although I really knew nothing about horses. There, in the stable, I was shown the pony and exclaimed, 'Oh! What a beauty.' 'Ah!' replied the old man, 'to them that *knows* a horse she *is* a beauty!'

I visited a mother whose baby was born one February night at 2 a.m. The night was bitterly cold and it seemed colder in the house than outside. The baby was four weeks premature and its condition was so poor that it was soon decided to transfer it to the maternity hospital so that it could be put in an incubator. The father, who was not very bright, told the whole neighbourhood that the baby had gone to hospital to be put in a *refrigerator*!

I remember an occasion when the Rector's daughter was

ASSISTANT: 'Is Madam expecting?'
SHOPPER: 'No, I'm jolly well CERTAIN.'

kindly doing some relief District Nursing. One of her patients was later heard to remark to a friend, 'Is that Miss —— from the Rectory a lady or a Nurse?'

Joyce Iliffe.

Change of Job

A lorry driver had arrived at the works with a load of material, and the foreman was checking it as it was loaded off. He thought the driver was looking a little fed up and so he asked him what was the matter.

'I am getting fed up with my job, and I think I should like to change it,' came the reply.

'What do you think you would like to do?'

'I dunno, really, I've always thought I should like to be an obstetrician.'

'You'd probably have to work a lot harder than you do now. You might have three or four babies to deal with a week.'

'That wouldn't worry me. I've been making three deliveries a *day* now for the past seven or eight years.'

A. C. Little.

The Discovery of Vaccination

It is interesting to find that very important and far-reaching results often stem from what, at the time, may seem some trivial and quite unimportant incident. It was in this way that the people of this country were finally freed from the scourge of smallpox which, up to the early part of the nineteenth century, had brought suffering, disfigurement, and death to thousands of people living in all levels of society. At one time there were 40,000 people yearly dying from smallpox in England, and those who managed to survive the disease were always scarred, blind, or insane.

The incident which started a train of thought which eventually led to the controlling of the disease, was simple enough. It came when Edward Jenner had finished his medical studies at St. George's Hospital and decided, in 1773, to go to Berkeley to set up in practice on his own account as an ordinary English country Doctor. It was during the visit of a milkmaid to a house at which Jenner was staying that he heard the milkmaid make a chance remark which kept worrying him for years. She was evidently discussing smallpox with one of her friends and Jenner heard her say, 'I cannot take that disease for I have had cowpox.'

For years Jenner could do little but think and talk about this remark, wondering to what possibilities it might lead him. He talked of it so much in the medical clubs which he attended, that his fellow-members soon became bored with him and made him a subject of ridicule. This, however, only served to spur him on and he began to tabulate his observations and carry out a number of experiments. Then, in 1796, he carried out an experiment which gave us vaccination. If the milkmaid's remark had been correct then, surely, he had only to give a person cow-pox and he would become immune from smallpox. With much daring, he vaccinated a boy of eight with lymph taken from the vesicles of cow-pox. A few weeks later he inoculated the same boy with smallpox but, much to his delight, the boy *did not* develop the dreaded disease, and he looked on this as a vindication of the experiments he had been carrying out for several years.

In 1798 he published an important pamphlet on vaccination giving full information of all the evidence he had been able to obtain since he first began to work on it. He described how, if a groom attended a horse which had a disease known then as 'grease', and got some of the discharge on his hands and then, without washing them, went off to milk a cow, he would most likely cause the cow to have cow-pox. When this happened, pustules would appear on the cow's nipples and later discharge. A milkmaid milking such a cow would herself take the disease, a condition lasting for no more than a few days.

'But,' wrote Jenner, 'what renders the cow-pox virus so singular, is that the person who has been thus affected is, for ever after, secure from the infection of smallpox.'

He cites the case of a woman who had suffered from cow-pox in 1765 but who, in 1792, nursed a child suffering from smallpox without, herself, catching the disease. He also mentions a lady of sixty-five, who had been ill with cow-pox when she was nine, but who suffered only a minor illness when he inoculated her with smallpox so many years afterwards.

Jenner was now sure that his theory of vaccination was proved, and he went to London assuming that people would flock to him to be vaccinated. To his bitter disappointment, however, no such thing happened and, instead, he was bitterly attacked by Doctors and clergy alike. The former had no faith in the new method, and the latter merely said that vaccination was both wicked and dangerous.

Jenner returned to Berkeley, and tried to persuade the 1,000 inhabitants of that district to allow themselves to be vaccinated. For a long time, however, they refused, many of them thinking that vaccination was the work of the Devil. Eventually Jenner persuaded twenty to come forward and these were followed by another twenty and then by a further seventy.

The result of this wholesale vaccination proved very successful, and from then on, Jenner's work was taken seriously. His first great triumph came in 1801, by which time over 100,000 persons had been vaccinated in England, when, after having treated the men of the Grand Fleet successfully, following a special request from the chiefs of the Navy, a special medal was struck to commemorate the historic occasion. In 1804, Napoleon Bonaparte also had a medal struck in his honour since, by this time, his methods were becoming popular and practised all over the world.

No better proof of his widespread fame can surely be given

than that the Indians in North America held a special meeting, at which their chief said: 'We shall not fail to teach our children to speak the name of Jenner; and to thank the Great Spirit for bestowing upon him so much wisdom and so much benevolence. We send with this, a belt and a string of Wampum in token of our acceptance of your precious gift; and we beseech the Great Spirit to take care of you in this world and in the land of Spirits.'

In Russia, the Dowager Empress requested the vaccination of a small girl, the first person to be treated in that country, and she had the girl named Vaccinoff, and set up sufficient funds to make her independent for life. She wrote a personal letter of thanks to Jenner, and with the letter sent him a diamond ring.

Jenner would undoubtedly have died a very rich man if he had kept the secret of his treatment to himself, but his love of humanity was much stronger than his love of money and he was quite willing that his methods should be fully understood everywhere.

He was not a rich man, and the time he had spent on his experiments meant that he had, of necessity, to neglect his practice as a Doctor. He felt, however, that he must have money if he was to carry on further with his work, and the many friends he now had in the medical profession urged him to press the Government for a grant. He followed their advice, and in 1802, the matter was discussed in the House of Commons. A grant of £10,000 was proposed, and two Members, Lords Grey and Wilberforce, proposed an amendment that the sum should be increased to £20,000. The amendment was defeated but the motion was easily passed, and during the next few years, further grants were made, making a total of £30,000. Jenner also received a gift of £7,000 from India, and further smaller gifts from all over the world. Thus he was able to carry on his work without any worry for lack of funds.

Altogether, Jenner was awarded some fifty diplomas, honours, and addresses, and several medals were struck to commemorate his discovery. He received an honorary degree of the University of Oxford, and was presented with the Freedom of many places including London, Edinburgh, Glasgow, Dublin, and Liverpool. He was also appointed Physician Extraordinary to the King.

Despite his fame, however, and the amount of time he had to spend on his various experiments, Jenner remained a true friend and benefactor to all, right up to the time of his death. He never refused to see a caller, be he rich or poor, and no matter whether it was early or late. The needy were always sure of his support if he was satisfied that the need was genuine.

When he was seventy-four, he braved a bitterly cold day to walk some miles to a neighbouring village to arrange a gift of coal to the poor. The following morning he was found insensible on the floor of his library, and the next day he died.

Such is the remarkable story of Edward Jenner, M.D., F.R.S., whose steadfast courage and devotion to his work, saved millions of lives and untold suffering. From it we can draw the very satisfying and reassuring thought that, probably at this very moment, there is a person devoted to medicine, somewhere in the world, who is discovering a method which will cure or ease the relatively small numbers of human conditions which are still baffling medical science.

L. C. Vaughan.

He Sure Was Hungry

Despite having had a tiresome illness for twenty-five years, I have been able to do some work, for most of the time, both as a Medical Missionary and a Ship's Surgeon.

In the former capacity I remember a party of Missionary friends of mine, travelling by horse over high Tibetan grassland, and for some reason the journey took longer than they had expected. For three days they were without food altogether. When they returned and reached the Mission Station, one of them said, 'I am so hungry the back of my front is touching the front of my back.'

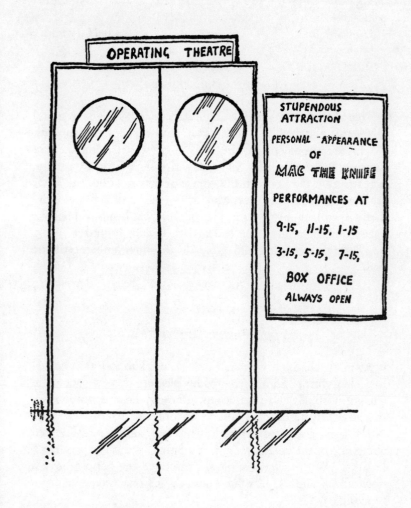

99

Whilst I was studying midwifery in Dublin, a clinical clerk sent word back to the Rotunda, saying, 'Baby dead, mother dying!' to which the reply was sent, 'Keep father alive until I bring help.'

R. A. H. Pearce.

Dropped Ball of Wool

The Vicar, a pleasant but inquisitive man, was going round the wards and having a brief chat with each of the patients. When he came to one patient, she was engrossed as usual, in her knitting, and the large ball of wool with which she was working, was lying on the floor. In the course of conversation, the Vicar asked me quietly, 'Let's see, Mrs. M—— had a dropped womb.' The patient had only a vague idea of what was being said but she gazed quickly around the bed and then said, brightly, 'Why, yes. I think it's fallen and gone on the floor underneath the bed.'

Betty J. Tresman.

Hardly what he Expected

As most television viewers I expect will know, I am married to a clergyman, and it is part of his pleasure to visit patients in various hospitals and institutions. One day he was visiting the sick in a private hospital run by an order of Roman Catholic Nuns. Somehow or other he lost his way, and as he wandered along one of the corridors he met a Sister. 'Is this the way out?' he asked. With never a smile she indicated the notice above a door which said, 'Operating Theatre'. 'It's one way,' she dryly remarked.

I was in hospital myself a few years ago for a short stay. One afternoon an old lady, looking very frail, was wheeled into the ward – female surgical – from the medical block where she had been having pre-operational treatment for several weeks. She was to have her operation the next day and was obviously very nervous. It was all made worse by the fact that she came from an extremely isolated Welsh farm and spoke and understood English only with great difficulty. We all did our best to reassure her but, I am afraid, without much success. Then, suddenly, in came two young Nurses who had been looking after her over 'on medical'. They propped her up and began chattering away in Welsh. The change was miraculous, and by the time they went to their supper, she looked a different person. I have often thought how nurses, with their sympathy and understanding, can be such a great help to patients under their care.

Two actual experiences I have heard from friends may be of interest.

A young V.A.D. was helping for the first time in a men's ward. One of her patient's rang the bell and asked her for a bottle. 'Certainly,' she said, 'I'll go and fill one for you at once!' It was only when she saw his amused expression that she realized he did not want a hot water bottle.

A young Probationer had been initiated into the mysteries of 'screens' and what went on behind them. One day the R.C. Chaplain came to her ward to take confession from one of his flock due to go down for an operation the next day. He asked her for screens to be put round the bed. Full of zeal and enthusiasm she rushed round and produced not only the screen but their usual accompaniment – a bed-pan!

Olive Stevens.

Some Miscellaneous Stories

A Nurse was preparing a bed next to a patient, and the patient asked if he was likely to have a mate. 'Yes,' said the Nurse, 'I think there is a case of thrombosis coming in soon.'

'That'll be a change,' said the patient, 'I'm getting a bit fed up with orange squash, in any case.'

*　　*　　*

Florence Nightingale always used a lamp, but it is said that the modern Nurse prefers a candle, so she can burn it at both ends.

*　　*　　*

An expectant father was visiting a London maternity home, and after he had spent a lot of time there, and done a lot of pacing about, a Nurse came to tell him joyfully that he was the father of a beautiful healthy-looking boy.

'But I don't think your wife has finished yet,' she said, 'it looks very much as though another baby is on the way. It probably won't come for a little while, and if I were you I think I should go off and have a drink, and come back later.'

The man went across the road to the public house and had a few drinks to celebrate the joyous occasion. Then, after a reasonable delay, he went back to the home and asked the Nurse if there had been any further developments. 'Yes,' she said, 'another baby has come but it still looks as if she hasn't finished yet. I think you had better go back and have another drink.'

The man returned to the public house and downed a few more drinks and, after much celebration, he did not feel too capable of going back to the home. He thought instead, he would use the phone and find out if there were any further developments. He dialled the number but somehow got it mixed up and got connected with Lord's Cricket Ground where a Test Match was being played.

'What's the position now?' he asked.

'Oh!' came the reply, 'it's all over now. The last two out were ducks.'

*　　*　　*

A patient had just been prepared for an operation and the Nurse said, 'Here comes the trolley down the ward.'

'That's good,' said the patient, 'I want to buy a few sweets.'

'It's not that sort of trolley,' replied the Nurse, 'it's one coming to take you to the theatre.'

'I'm going to see a show, am I?' said the patient. 'That's good. Do you think I'll come away laughing?'

'I don't know about that,' said the Nurse, 'but I'm sure you'll come away in stitches.'

*　　*　　*

Sister was showing a visitor round a sick ward of male patients. 'Are you never worried,' asked the visitor 'that some of these men might make a pass at you?'

'No,' said the Sister, 'they are all too ill for that.'

Then she started suddenly, looked around, and said to a patient immediately behind her, 'So you are beginning to get a bit better are you?'

*　　*　　*

A Doctor was called out early one dark evening to a farm deep in the country where a woman was expecting a baby. He knew that the local Midwife was ill and that he could expect no help from her. He wondered if there would be anyone at the farmhouse who could help him if he needed it.

When he arrived he learned that the husband was out somewhere and that the only other occupant in the house was the woman's father, an ageing man he knew as 'Jock'. The only illumination in the room came from a paraffin lamp and he informed Jock that he might need him at some time to hold the lamp so that he would be better able to see what he was doing.

He examined the woman and could see that things might soon be happening. He told Jock to be prepared and to come into the bedroom immediately he called him. It was not long before the call came, and Jock shuffled in and held the lamp whilst a bonny baby boy was delivered. The doctor told him he could manage now, and sent him back to the kitchen. Not long afterwards, however, a groan came from the bed, and it was evident that a second baby was on the way. Jock was called back, and held the lamp whilst the doctor went through his performance again. As soon as it was over, Jock returned once more to the kitchen.

The Doctor thought everything was finished now, but it was not too long before he had to shout for Jock again. The old man came rambling in, grasped the lamp and held it up, as he had done twice before. Then he turned to the Doctor and said: 'Hi, Doctor, do you think it's the light that's attracting them?'

*　　*　　*

A dwarf was making love to an attractive woman, when her husband came home suddenly and unexpectedly. Without a moment's hesitation, the dwarf threw open the window and jumped out.

Taken to hospital, he was carefully patched up and made comfortable. When this had all been done, he turned to the Doctor, and asked what injuries he had sustained.

'You're very lucky,' said the Doctor, 'all you have got is a broken arm, a broken leg, two broken fingers, and a cracked skull.'

'What do you mean by "lucky"?' asked the dwarf.

'Well,' said the Doctor, 'you were lucky you did not have to jump out of a window in a house – only in a bungalow.'

H. C. T.

Pity the Postman

This is a true story about a dear old man in a Geriatric Ward in which I was serving at the time.

He asked me to post a letter for him to one of his relatives, and I, of course, readily agreed. On looking at the unstamped envelope, however, I read:

> Mrs. Jones,
>> Box Cottage,
>>> Up the Hill,
>>>> Forget the address.

You can imagine my surprise on reading this, but many of us had a good laugh about it. One of the Nurses suggested I should send it to one of the Women's Magazines asking for Readers' Letters, and I was thrilled when I received a fiver for it.

B. Westley.

The Great John Hunter

The pages of medical history contain the names of many men, so devoted to their calling, that the magnitude of their devotion is sometimes hard to believe. One such is John Hunter who died, as a result of his personal pursuit of knowledge, on 16 October, 1793. He had deliberately given himself a dangerous disease, in order that he might be the better able to study it, from which he eventually succumbed.

He is gratefully remembered as the greatest surgeon of all time, and he spent many years studying anatomy and pathology, and during the course of his work made several important discoveries which laid the foundation for the scientific surgery we know today.

He was never very well but thought nothing of working full out for twenty hours a day. He would often rise at 4 a.m. or 5 a.m. and go on working until the early hours of the following morning. He considered that four or five hours' sleep was all he ever needed. On one occasion, he is said to have ordered one of his students to 'come to me tomorrow morning early, as soon after four as you can'. The student obeyed the instruction, only to find him already busy – dissecting beetles!

His students came to love him, and in time, affectionately referred to him as 'the old man'. To begin with, however, his lectures were poorly attended. He was the first to hold classes of the kind in surgery, and there was much opposition, from other prominent members of the profession, to this novel innovation. It is said that, on one occasion, he found it necessary to bring a skeleton into the classroom in order that he might address the class in the normal way as 'gentlemen'.

Hunter had a passion for dissecting the bodies of humans and animals alike, and his house was always cluttered up with corpses and skeleton 'freaks', and numerous animals awaiting attention, and still very much alive.

Hunter's knowledge and important discoveries were all the more remarkable in that he had received but a poor education in his early years. His writing and spelling remained abominable throughout his life, and he was unable to follow properly the work of his foreign contemporaries. Moreover, he knew practically nothing of chemistry and physics and the microscope had not yet come to play an important part in the field of research. He was always aware of his shortcomings but was never doubtful of his ability. On one occasion he is said to have told his colleagues at St. George's Hospital that, although he regarded himself as a pigmy in knowledge, he was really a giant in medical understanding compared with any one of them.

Privately he was a man, like so many devoted to their calling, who was generous beyond compare. He would never accept fees from patients whom he felt were unable to afford them, and he made it a rule always to treat clergymen, authors, and artists for nothing. Wealthy patients could expect none of his preference, and he would often keep them waiting whilst he first attended to working men who could ill afford to lose the time off work necessary in order to come and consult him.

In the course of some forty years of work, and the expenditure of more than £20,000, Hunter gathered together a wonderful anatomical and surgical museum, and this was acquired by the nation after his death. It has provided a mine of invaluable information for surgeons ever since.

T. F. R.

My Most Amusing Experiences

Before my marriage, I spent seven years in nursing, and whilst in training at a large hospital in Devon, I experienced the following amusing episodes.

I was half-way through the early morning bed-pan round, and had finished one side of the ward. Half-way down the opposite side sat 'Gran' looking very perky and expectant. After a while, I said, 'Have you finished then, Gran?' to which she replied, 'No, dear, I'm waiting for some hot water to wash my feet in!'

Whilst on night duty once – the time about 4.30 a.m. – I was 'doing the backs'. We had only two blue light bulbs fixed high in the ceiling as it was wartime. I put my hand into the patient's locker to rub soap on to my hands. I found the soap, as I thought, and started rubbing the patient's back vigorously. Then I began to realize that something was wrong – the soap felt unusually sticky. I brought a torch, and to my horror I discovered I'd used a Mars bar instead of soap!

An elderly male patient I once had usually lit up his pipe once in the night. This particular night he seemed a little restless, and so I asked him what the trouble was. He replied, 'I think I'll go out to the back, m'dear.' I left him to do so, and after a while, I returned and asked, 'Everything all right, Grandad?' 'No,' he said, 'I thought you were going out first to warm the seat!'

An elderly lady patient was being examined by a Consulting Physician who was very hard of hearing. He asked her in a loud voice, 'What's the trouble, Mrs.——?' 'It's the twinge, sir,' she explained. His reply was, 'Well, madam, I don't know how you manage to have twins at your age.'

A male patient was asked to supply a specimen and given instructions as to the correct area of the building to which he should take it. After some time, when he had not put in an appearance, a nurse was sent to locate him. She looked just outside the Out-Patients' entrance, just in case – and there she saw a man with a bewildered countenance, a trilby hat on his head, carrying a specimen along the pavement!

Mrs. Margaret White.

The Story of Penicillin

Of all the many wonderful discoveries of medical science, throughout the last two hundred years or so, none can surely compare with the discovery and development of penicillin. To-day the name of this drug has become a household word, and millions of people throughout the world undoubtedly owe their continued existence to it.

Most people are aware that the accidental discovery which finally led to the manufacture of penicillin on a commercial scale, was made by Sir Alexander Fleming as early as 1928. It was not until some ten years afterwards, however, when a brilliant young biochemist named Dr. Ernest Chain, a refugee from Hitler, walked into the laboratory at an Oxford hospital and joined the department run by Professor Howard Florey, that serious investigation into Fleming's discovery was made. Neither of these men had planned the work on which they were later to become engaged, but it was soon apparent that both had been nursing a long curiosity in the papers which Fleming had published following his discovery. It was natural, therefore, that they should decide to carry out investigations and experiments which the Fleming discovery suggested might be worth carrying out.

In passing, it is interesting to note the different backgrounds of these three men, who were later to be awarded the Nobel Prize, and in doing so, to reflect upon the world-wide brotherhood which happily exists among scientists. Fleming was a farm boy from Ayrshire, Chain a refugee from Germany who had worked in a Berlin hospital, and Florey an Australian.

Alexander Fleming was born in a lonely farmhouse above Darvel, close to the borders of Ayrshire, Renfrewshire, and Lanarkshire. He and his two brothers, for several years, walked four miles to and from a village school, and it must have been a very tiresome journey sometimes in winter. Later he went to Kilmarnock Academy. His elder brother went to London as an ophthalmic surgeon, and Alexander went to live with him, still young enough to go to school. Leaving school, he spent several years as a clerk in a shipping office, but all the time he was hankering after a medical career, which it seemed he would never be able to follow. Then, suddenly, he came into a legacy which was sufficient to enable him to take up medical training, and he managed to get into St. Mary's Hospital Medical School as a student. As a student, he was brilliant and won many prizes and scholarships, and graduated finally with honours in physiology, pharmacology, medicine, pathology, forensic medicine, and hygiene.

Fleming's discovery, which has finally resulted in the manufacture of the drug penicillin in a convenient form, on an enormous scale, and at comparatively low cost, was nothing but a pure 'accident'. Moreover, it was an 'accident' which occurred when Fleming was actually miles away from his laboratory. It was in September 1928, when Fleming was taking a rare holiday in Suffolk, pottering about Barton Mills in flannel trousers and tweed jacket and enjoying his time fishing in the mill stream.

Fleming's main work consisted of smearing various germs on to suitably prepared plates and allowing them to grow until they could readily be studied under a microscope. Such smearings are known as moulds and, under properly controlled conditions, multiply at a very fast rate. Many grow into a spotted mould, not unlike that which is familiar to all of us when it occurs on the surface of an open pot of jam. Whilst Fleming was away, a spore of fungus – nothing more than a little bit of fluff – somehow drifted on to one of the plates on which he was breeding germs. The particular culture was that of the microbe which causes common boils. What Fleming was amazed to see was that the area surrounding the foreign body was different from the rest and that, in fact, all the germs within it were dead. Fleming identified the germ which had given this extraordinary effect and then cultivated the mould and gave the name 'penicillin' to the substance exuded by it. As was natural, Fleming felt he had to play about with the mould and carry out extensive experiments. But he soon got stuck. He had not been trained as a chemist and the possibilities connected with his discovery were not apparent to him. He was, he has said, 'very much more interested in other things than in penicillin'. As a true scientist, however, he made very detailed notes of the events which led up to his discovery and on the experiments which he followed out afterwards. It was not until ten years afterwards that these notes were studied seriously by Florey and Chain, two bio-chemists at Oxford, and carefully planned experiments were carried on.

By 1940 it had been found that penicillin had the power to prevent the growth of certain germs due to the substance which the mould manufactured. Both here and in America, the fact was quickly grasped that a drug of this description might have very beneficial and valuable results if used on war casualties, and the effort to purify the drug and step up production was intensified. It was soon realized how useful it was to have a drug which would kill germs but which, at the same time, would be harmless to the cells of the body.

One of the early experiments of Chain and Florey was to give an infection to fifty white mice, and then to treat half of them with penicillin and to leave the other half alone. The scientists watched all night to see the result of this experiment, and by the morning, all the untreated mice were dead, and those which had been given penicillin were frisking about. Chain has said that the result was 'quite outstanding'. 'Even more so,' he has said, 'since, in this experiment, there was only one per cent penicillin and ninety-nine per cent impurities.'

From here the chemists went on to purify the drug and they realized how potent it could be in a purified form, when only one per cent had already produced such amazing results. Fleming was naturally very interested himself in what was going on, and he went to Oxford to examine the results. He was very gratified to see what results had been achieved so many years after his discovery. His only worry now was that the drug might be used too extensively, and he warned that over-use might reduce its effectiveness in patients who were given large doses on one occasion, and who might require similar treatment at some later date. He was amazed at the number of diseases which could profit from its use. He was once asked, 'Is this stuff of yours any good for a hang-over?' He replied, 'Heavens, no, it's not *that* good.'

Fleming, Florey, and Chain are the great names connected with penicillin, but a person who does not come into the picture as often, and as prominently, as she should, is Ethel Florey, Dr. Howard Walter Florey's wife. She, herself, was qualified professionally, and received a medical degree from the University of Adelaide, at which university her husband had also studied, and gained a scholarship to England as a Rhodes Scholar.

Dr. Howard Florey came home from his laboratory late one day, worn out and tired, and not a little worried. His team had succeeded in making small quantities of a yellow-brown powder containing penicillin, and this had been used, with unfailing results, on a number of animals. It was, however, virtually unknown on human beings. Before there was clinical evidence of its human value, no pharmaceutical house could be expected to risk the large sum necessary to produce it in worth-while quantities, but, in wartime, doctors were in such short supply that who could be found to carry out this special work? That was Dr Florey's big worry. He talked the matter over with his wife, and after remaining silent for some time, she suddenly said, 'I'll do it!'

Florey now had to persuade some of the Oxford hospitals to allow his wife to administer the drug to suitable patients. In 1942 she was given a small quantity of the precious powder – not what in all, today, would be considered an adequate dose for a single patient – and she made up her meagre ration in solution and ointment, and put her preparation in sterilized bottles and jars. Then she set forth on her momentous mission.

She decided that she would concentrate first on surface infections, where the results could be easily observed. She concentrated on ulcers and abscesses, and she was thrilled to find that, in all cases, the offending germs cleared quickly, and the flesh healed cleanly.

Discussing the results with her husband, she soon realized that the biggest hope for penicillin was in its successful treatment of infections deep within the body. Injections had already been made into veins, but difficulty had been found in maintaining an effective level of the drug in the blood. The next thing, then, was obviously to inject into the muscles.

About this time, a young woman was admitted to the Radcliffe Infirmary suffering from haemorrhage and severe pelvic infection, brought about by a self-induced abortion. Her life was ebbing away fast. Ethel gave her what were, in those days, enormous doses of penicillin twice a day for six days. To everyone's amazement, the girl completely recovered, and there were no ill-effects from the drug.

The value of the new drug was now beginning to become widely appreciated, and shortly after this incident, Ethel was called to a two-month-old baby whose spine was twisted and who had a severe bone infection. She started penicillin treatment immediately, and by the ninth day there was a definite improvement, and the baby had gained a few ounces in weight. Six

ANGRY POSTMAN: 'Your dog has just bitten me, missus.'
HOUSEHOLDER: 'Thank you for telling me, I'll take him down to the vet.
and have him disinfected straight away.'

months later, the baby's spine was almost straight and, healthy looking and lively, the baby was handed back to his parents.

With each new triumph, penicillin became much more in demand, and supplies woefully inadequate. Things were so bad, in fact, that the drug was actually collected from the urine of patients who had been given it, purified, and used again. In 1943, *The Lancet* was able to announce that techniques had been developed for administering the drug intramuscularly, intro-venously, by mouth, in ointment, and on dressings. And, in a paper never given to the over-use of words, said of Florey's work that it 'leaves no doubt about the potential value of this bacteriostatic agent'.

The war and its many casualties focused attention on this 'potential value', and pharmaceutical firms in America, with Government aid, went in for the production of penicillin in a big way.

On D-Day, Ethel Florey had her own unit, administering penicillin in one of England's largest hospitals. In this connection alone, it is claimed that the drug saved 3,000 Normandy casual-ties from gas gangrene. Its use also enabled surgeons to patch up hundreds of mangled limbs, thus avoiding amputation.

The Americans soon put their genius for large-scale production to work, and they soon came up with a new system which would enable the drug to be mass-produced. By 1943, in fact, they were producing 800 million units a month. Early in 1944 the Ministry of Supply was convinced that mass production was not only desirable, but possible, and, calling in experts, they spent one and a quarter million pounds setting up the largest penicillin factory in the world at Speke, near Liverpool.

The factory covered a twelve-acre plot, with an extensive group of laboratories housed in eight huge blocks. A breeding stock of 120 mice and twenty-two rabbits were shipped to this country from U.S.A. in the bomb-bay of a bomber, and this original stock quickly grew into many thousands. These animals have been used to test every batch of penicillin before it has been passed fit for human administration. This, however, has been only one of several tests to make certain of the drug's purity and efficacy.

Such, briefly, is the story of penicillin, one of the wonders of the medical world, and certainly its biggest life-saver.

T. T. H.

A Surprising Drink

A Doctor looked into his waiting-room to call the next patient, and was surprised to find her and her friend shrieking with unseemly laughter. The patient had just discovered that a small gin bottle had been lifted from her wicker shopping basket, whilst she had been shopping, prior to coming to the surgery. It was the only bottle she had been able to find at home in which to put the 'specimen' for which the Doctor had asked!

G. S. Kennett.

Plaster Casts

A very large and stately lady, the pinnacle of local county society, consulted me about her painful feet.

She accepted my diagnosis of flat feet, and it was arranged that plaster casts be made. This procedure took place in a long drawing-room, at one end of which she was seated in a chair, and invited to put her feet into two pudding basins half-filled with wet plaster of Paris. After a suitable interval, to allow the plaster to set, I asked her to lift her feet gently from the moulds. To my alarm, both feet rose in the air with the basins firmly attached. She rose to her full height and took a tentative step forward, but with no benefit. Panic seized her. She broke into a shambling trot down the room, followed by her lady companion and myself. The effect was that of a huge scared duck making for its pond. She was assisted back to her chair, but some time elapsed before I returned with a mallet and cold-chisel to get her out of a very awkward situation.

This was one of my first orthopaedic efforts, and this particular method was one which I never employed again.

Country Doctor.

Ministry Howlers

I have seen many examples of unconscious humour which frequently come into the hands of various officials in different departments of the Ministries. Here are a few of those I have liked the best.

'Sorry I have been so long filling in the form, but I have been in bed with my baby two weeks, and did not know it was running out until the milkman told me.'

'I am unable to get sick pay. I have six children, can you tell me why this is? I now have a seventh child. What are you going to do about it?'

'Dear Sir, As you wanted, I am forwarding my marriage certificate and two children, one of which you will see is a mistake.'

'Please send me a form for cheap milk. I have a baby two months old, and I did not know anything about it until a friend told me.'

'In reply to your letter, I am sending my marriage certificate and five children. I did have six, but one died. This was baptized on half a sheet of note paper by the Revd. Jones.'

'I have a child nearly two years of age, and am looking forward to an increase in November. Hoping this meets with your approval.'

'In accordance with your instructions I gave birth to a baby girl three days ago.'

'I am in urgent need of my sick pay. I have been in bed with the Doctor for a week, and he don't seem to be doing me much good. If things don't alter, I shall have to get a new one.'

'Please send me form for supply of milk for having children at cheap rate.'

A Health Visitor, visiting a mother regarding the illness of one of her children, was greeted with the remark, 'I don't know what it is, but it is nothing "*affectionate*".'

'I have a baby eighteen months old, thanking you for the same.'

Civil Servant.

Nursing Incidents

Here are a few of the many humorous incidents I have come across during my years of nursing.

Two Nurses, who were identical twins, worked in the same hospital. A psychiatrist visited a men's ward, did a round, and said good-bye to the Nurse in charge there. Then he went to a women's ward and found, as he thought, the same Nurse as the one he had just left. It puzzled him how she could have arrived so quickly, until the Sister explained that the Nurses were twins. 'Oh, dear,' he said, 'for one moment I thought I ought to examine myself!'

A patient once declared after having had a rectal lavage, 'Oh, dear, I feel all washed out!'

There is a rule in hospital that no Night Nurse, on a men's ward, should go off duty without first clearing away the urinal bottles from the several lockers. I remember that, on one occasion when there were several of these, the Nurse lined them up in order, as near to the sluice as possible, but without taking them outside the ward. Her colleague had gone out for a few minutes, and it was also a rule that no ward should be left unattended in case anything happened. The nurse could not complete the operation, therefore, until her colleague returned but, much to her consternation, the Night Sister came in unexpectedly and saw all the bottles, lined up near the door. She looked in horror at the sight, and then shrieked, 'Nurse, whatever are they all doing there?' The Nurse looked vacant for a moment and then innocently replied, 'Oh, they are just queueing up to go outside!'

L. Fox.

Another Apple

Judy, who was three, had been badly scalded, and the District Nurse was visiting her twice a day. One day when she called, she found her mother trying to tempt a poor appetite.

'Eat an apple,' her mother said.

'No!'

'Come on, my dear. They say an apple a day keeps the Doctor away.'

The child took the apple and, after gazing at it for a minute, said hopefully, 'If I eat another, will it keep the District Nurse away as well?'

Ex-District Nurse.

Bring my Slipper

During a varied nursing career I have witnessed many amusing incidents. Here are just three of them.

Old 'Pappa' was suffering from a heart complaint, and so was confined to bed. Having the urge to answer the call of nature, he called, 'Nurse, bring me my slipper.' 'Dad, you can't get out of bed, so you don't need your slipper,' replied the Nurse (at that time an inexperienced member of the profession). 'But Nurse, I need the slipper.' 'I'm sorry, Dad, you can't have your slippers, as the Doctor said you are not to get up.' 'But Nurse,' roared the patient, 'I need to *use* it.' The little Nurse then tumbled to what he meant and turning round to the desk, noticed the Staff Nurse in fits of laughter.

A young Nurse was sent to the bed of a patient who had just been examined by the Doctor. 'Nurse,' said the Doctor. 'wash that man's umbilicus.' The Nurse dutifully disappeared behind the screen and started to search for something, but had no idea what. Thinking the job was done, the Ward Sister came to investigate, and one can imagine her surprise to find the Nurse on her hands and knees looking in the patient's locker. 'What are you looking for, Nurse?' she asked. Nurse, feeling embarrassed, stood up and tried to look dignified. 'Please, Sister, I am looking for the man's Ummmmm.' 'You mean his umbilicus, Nurse?' 'Yes, Sister,' replied the Nurse, with a relieved grin on her face. Needless to say she was enlightened as to where to find it, immediately, and she has always been able to locate it since.

When I was first appointed to the Mission field, I was asked to be responsible for midwifery, which meant being on call for every case which happened to be in labour, so I could guide the students in knowing what to look for and how to care for the patient. Needless to say, there were many really funny reports from the wards in the middle of the night. I had taught them to call me when the patient was 'fully dilated' and, or when, the

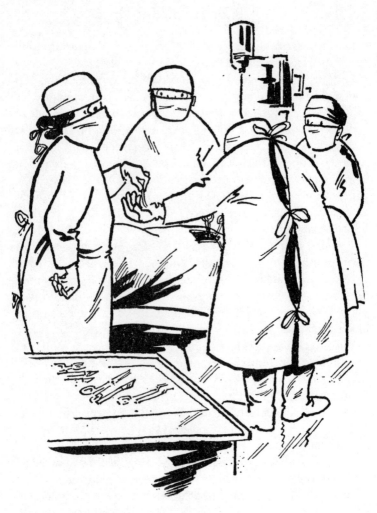

SURGEON: 'Clip, Nurse.'
THEATRE SISTER: 'Sister, doctor.'
SURGEON: 'Mister, Sister.'

patient was ready to 'bear down'. They had heard me say to the mums, 'Come on now, push!' This night a rap came on the window just under the head of my bed, and a voice said, 'Please, Sister, the patient is fully delighted and is pushing off!' I thought I would explode, but there being no one awake to share the joke, I quickly got up, pulled on my housecoat and ran to the ward to deliver the baby.

Beryl M. Turtill (Nigeria).

The Poor Lady Almoner

Here is a perfectly true experience which is quite amusing. My husband, Harry S. Pepper, slipped in our village street and badly dislocated his right shoulder. He was taken to our Cottage Hospital, and there being no private rooms available at the time, he was put into a bed in the men's ward. The next day, a real 'rough diamond' (whom, for the sake of non-identification, I will call 'Smithy') was admitted to the same ward.

A day later, after a gentle but firm remonstration from my husband that certain somewhat revolting habits *must* be curbed when in a ward with other men, 'Smithy' completely succumbed to my husband and, for ever after, addressed him as 'Sir'!

The principal thing about 'Smithy' was that – cure his manners maybe temporarily – one could not cure within a matter of ten days his lifetime habit of using swear words much as we use 'and', 'if', and 'but'! Even so, cutting out the swear words – which are not printable, anyhow – I think the following makes a very amusing story, and it is perfectly true.

'Smithy' – by now a firm friend of my husband – was telling him one day of his troubles in another hospital, and of how he was advised to see the Lady Almoner, who would certainly be able to help him. 'So,' said 'Smithy', 'I goes to see this 'ere Lady Almoner. Cor, Mr. Pepper, sir, what a something, something, so-and-so *she* was! 'Ow *Lord* Almoner puts up with '*er*, I don't so-and-so know!'

Bits and Pieces

The Chairman of the Health Committee was giving one of his usual reports to the Council, and during this stated that the Medical Officer had given the death rate for the previous year as 9·8 per 1,000 of the population. One of the members, showing his ignorance, asked: 'What does 9·8 mean?' 'It simply means,' said the Chairman, 'that during last year, nine persons out of every thousand actually died, and eight were at the point of death.'

* * *

A man of about thirty-five was examined by his Doctor, and when the Doctor had finished his examination, he said, 'I'm sorry, but I'm afraid you will have to give up either smoking or women.' The patient thought for a few seconds, and then he said, 'I think I'll give up smoking. I can always smoke when I get older.'

* * *

A Librarian who had issued a book called *The Angel* to a borrower, later received a letter from him explaining that he could not return the book as 'the angel has been sent to the Sanitary Authorities for disinfection'.

* * *

Have you ever thought that a Specialist is the only person who can ask a strange lady to take off all her clothes, get her to do it without any trouble, and then demand a fee from her husband?

* * *

A District Nurse was attending a mother with a new baby, and found that the baby had two of its toes joined together. 'I will see the Doctor,' she said, 'and he will make arrangements for the toes to be separated.' 'Oh, no,' gasped the mother, 'what God has joined, I will let no man put asunder.'

Anon.

Index

125